John McTiernan

John McTiernan

The Rise and Fall of an Action Movie Icon

LARRY TAYLOR

McFarland & Company, Inc., Publishers
Jefferson, North Carolina

LIBRARY OF CONGRESS CATALOGUING-IN-PUBLICATION DATA

Names: Taylor, Larry, 1981– author.
Title: John McTiernan : the rise and fall of an action movie icon / Larry Taylor.
Description: Jefferson, North Carolina : McFarland & Company, Inc., Publishers, 2018 | Includes bibliographical references and index.
Identifiers: LCCN 2018022643 | ISBN 9781476673165 (softcover : acid free paper) ∞
Subjects: LCSH: McTiernan, John. | Motion picture producers and directors—United States—Biography. | LCGFT: Biographies.
Classification: LCC PN1998.3.M39782 T39 2018 | DDC 791.4302/32092 [B] —dc23
LC record available at https://lccn.loc.gov/2018022643

BRITISH LIBRARY CATALOGUING DATA ARE AVAILABLE

ISBN (print) 978-1-4766-7316-5
ISBN (ebook) 978-1-4766-3233-9

No part of this book may be reproduced or transmitted in any form or by any means, electronic or mechanical, including photocopying or recording, or by any information storage and retrieval system, without permission in writing from the publisher.

Front cover: John McTiernan shooting the 1987 film *Predator* (photograph courtesy of 20th Century–Fox); background images © 2018 iStock

Printed in the United States of America

McFarland & Company, Inc., Publishers
   Box 611, Jefferson, North Carolina 28640
      www.mcfarlandpub.com

For Dad

Acknowledgments

There are so many people to thank for the very existence of this book. My mother ... my dad ... my friends... But I would never have been able to finish this were it not for the love, support and patience of my wife, Brandy, the greatest wife and mother any hapless dreamer like me could ask for.

Table of Contents

Introduction	1

Part I: Euros and Nomads
1. The European Influence	11
2. *Nomads*	17

Part II: Welcome to the Jungle
3. *Predator*	23
4. The Van Damme Experiment	29
5. A Survival Story	34
6. *Predator* and "Taking the Piss Out" of '80s Machismo	38
7. John McTiernan, Man of Action	42

Part III: Yippee Ki Yay
8. *Nothing Lasts Forever*	47
9. An Ode to Joy, Not Terror	54
10. Nakatomi Nuance	59
11. The New Action Template	63

Part IV: The Connery Years
12. The Clancy Phenomenon	69
13. There Will Never Be Another *Red October*	78
14. Finding the *Medicine Man*	81

Table of Contents

PART V: TOO BIG TO FAIL?

15. *Extremely Violent* — 89
16. *Last Action Hero*: Ahead of Its Time or Timeless Disaster? — 97
17. "Simon Says" — 104
18. No McTiernan, No Real McClane — 112

Part VI: Highs and Lows

19. Trouble at Home — 117
20. The Norse Debacle — 119
21. In Defense of *The 13th Warrior* — 125
22. Silver Lining — 128
23. The Catherine Banning Affair — 137

Part VII: Downward Spiral

24. *Rollerball* — 143
25. Dodging a Bullet — 153
26. *Basic* — 155

Part VIII: Pellicano

27. The Pellicano Problem — 163
28. The Political Prosecutions of Karl Rove — 171
29. Keep Moving — 174
30. Inmate #43029-112 — 177
31. The Legal Mountain — 182
32. Burning Bridges — 188
33. The Comeback Kid? — 191
34. Nothing Lasts Forever — 194

Chapter Notes — 201
Bibliography — 208
Index — 211

Introduction

John McTiernan came along in a time of American action moviemaking where mercenary directors churned out superstar-led blockbusters, their visual stamp on the finished product a faint watermark in comparison to the sweaty biceps dominating the big screen. The eye behind the camera was far less important than the ego in front during the overwhelming success of the 1980s actioner; Joseph Zito, George P. Cosmatos, Mark Lester, John Irvin, and the like were filmmakers dwarfed by the larger-than-life personalities for whom their films were made. Names like Arnold Schwarzenegger, Sylvester Stallone, and Chuck Norris on the marquee rendered the name at the bottom of the poster practically irrelevant.

Because Hollywood in the 1980s was an industry in transition, a business shifting its model from the free-wheeling creative American filmmaking in the preceding decade—influenced by European New Wave movements—to a more controlled, packaged studio model.

The 1970s were, and still are, the zenith of creative brilliance and ingenuity in Hollywood. It was a wild and unchecked time of independent cinema, experimentation, brought on by the growing influence of European filmmaking style and technique spurred by the French New Wave.

François Truffaut, Jean-Luc Godard, and Jacques Rivette are only a few filmmakers who were pioneers of the French New Wave movement in the 1950s and '60s. Their films, and the films of their peers, shifted the approach to directing and telling a story, focusing on location shoots, current events, and inventive new camera angles. It was a substantial shift from the Hollywood studio model, and, before long, the French New Wave found its way to American shores.

The sea change in Hollywood unofficially began with Arthur Penn's 1967 crime picture *Bonnie and Clyde*—heavily guided by the works of

Introduction

Godard and Truffaut—which turned into an avalanche of great American movies from new directors that would stretch across the entirety of the 1970s.[1] William Friedkin gave us *The French Connection* and *The Exorcist* in 1971 and 1973, respectively; Francis Ford Coppola created the epic *Godfather* saga (or at least two of the three chapters) with a brilliant paranoid thriller, *The Conversation*, sandwiched in between; and Martin Scorsese blew audiences away with *Mean Streets* and, later in the decade, *Taxi Driver*.

There was the blossoming career of a hyper-stylistic Hitchcock devotee named Brian De Palma, who directed the psychological thriller *Sisters* and the idiosyncratic rock opera *The Phantom of the Paradise* in the early '70s before announcing his arrival with the critical and commercial success of *Carrie*—an adaptation of Stephen King's first novel, which would subsequently launch King's career. At the same time there was the minimalist masterpiece, Peter Bogdanovich's *The Last Picture Show*, the naturalistic works of John Cassavetes's films, and there was a young kid from Cincinnati named Steven Spielberg who would birth the very notion of the summer movie season with a story about a killer shark.

The success of Spielberg's *Jaws*, followed by the culture-altering tidal wave that was George Lucas's *Star Wars* phenomenon two years later, would redirect studio resources to the hot months on the calendar. Summer was the place to make their money for the year with big movies and epic scope, and the fall was the place on the calendar for more "serious" fare.

All the while, writers, directors, and actors continued churning out masterpieces left and right, working outside of the system and crafting their own stories despite the push back from any Old World studio executives. Eventually, these executives and moneymen backed off when the success of these "New Hollywood" films became too great to ignore.

The flashpoint of New Hollywood's success may have been *The Deer Hunter*, Michael Cimino's controversial 1978 Vietnam War film that won five Academy Awards in the spring of 1979, including Best Picture and Director for Cimino. *The Deer Hunter*, which told the story of a group of blue-collar Pennsylvania steelworkers and friends who were shipped off to war, was a challenging film filled with tremendous darkness, shot with an eye towards naturalism and saddled with a litany of complaints regarding the one-dimensional, racist characterization of the Viet Cong in an extended scene where murderous Vietnamese soldiers force captured Americans into a game of Russian roulette. Jane Fonda, whose own Vietnam

Introduction

John McTiernan overseeing the *Predator* (20th Century–Fox, 1987) shoot.

film *Coming Home* was a competitor of *The Deer Hunter*, was the most outspoken opponent of Cimino's film.

Regardless of whatever controversy may have polluted the film's reception, *The Deer Hunter* marked the beginning of the end of boundless '70s creativity; and nobody realized it at the time.

Michael Cimino may have created one of the last great American movies of the 1970s, but he also became infamously tied to the symbolic demise of New Hollywood just two years later. His 1980 Western epic *Heaven's Gate* was one of the first troubled productions to spill more newspaper ink about the chaos behind the cameras than the film itself. Cimino's passion project initially built up a $36 million budget in a time when the average was $12 million; when the dust settled and he turned in the finished product, *Heaven's Gate* was a bloated, unfocused five-hour mess that United Artists could do nothing with. A runtime like that would make it practically impossible to market and sell. And beyond that, theaters in 1980 only had a few screens, some only one; showing a five-hour Western was almost logistically impossible. United Artists forced Cimino to do extensive cutting on the film, and eventually the theatrical version came in under three hours. It still wasn't enough to fix what ailed the story.

Heaven's Gate was a colossal disaster for Cimino and United Artists, not even reaching $3.5 million, less than 10 percent of its massive budget (which had ballooned to $44 million after all the bills were counted). The financial calamity was a huge black eye for United Artists. Over the years it was rumored to be the reason for United Artists' initial downfall, but those are erroneous claims. Transamerica, the parent company of United Artists, wrote off the losses from *Heaven's Gate*, and the company was eventually sold to MGM.

Nevertheless, *Heaven's Gate* was also enough of a cautionary tale for the rest of the studios that they began reining in the wild, creative personalities who had made the 1970s film output so great. The money wasn't flowing as freely anymore as studios sought to have more say over the products they were endorsing. While it may have corrected the monetary side of things, creativity took a back seat to more controlled environments.

This new restraint from the higher-ups, coupled with the changing ideologies in the country—Ronald Reagan's presidential victory and his "Morning in America" mentality, cultivating a hedonistic spend-first attitude in the U.S.—pointed studios in certain directions to try and match the collective disposition of society. Bleary-eyed paranoia and distrust of the government was no longer the mood of the country, and the entire film industry began to shift accordingly, especially in their approach to action films.

There were plenty of action movies prior to the 1980s. The cops-and-robbers serials of the 1930s and '40s, James Cagney and *White Heat*, adventure films like *Treasure of the Sierra Madre*, the James Bond series beginning in the '60s, and Steve McQueen classics like *Bullitt* and *The Great Escape*, all helped define action cinema in the young history of Hollywood. The '70s had their own share of action, namely the invention of Dirty Harry Callahan and the aforementioned birth of the summer blockbuster. Bruce Lee was brought to America via *The Way of the Dragon* and *Enter the Dragon* in 1972 and 1973, respectively.

First Blood, Sylvester Stallone's 1982 maiden voyage with the John Rambo character, signaled the end of an era. It was a big action movie and a sizeable hit, but it was one of the last of its kind, a leftover relic from the '70s when that aforementioned government distrust and cynicism pushed aside creative voices. The story of a disenfranchised army vet and a villainous authority figure wasn't jibing with the zeitgeist as Ronald Reagan promised greater prosperity. This was a new dawn, a new day, and American audiences wanted heroes and winners, warriors and patriots. When it was time for the inevitable sequel to *First Blood*, the John Rambo

Introduction

character was rearranged to fit in with the jingoistic resurgence in the country. Stallone reprised the role in 1985's *Rambo: First Blood Part II*, and John Rambo was no longer a broken man, a drifter suffering from Post-Traumatic Stress Disorder and tossed aside by those he fought for, but a quietly rehabilitated, chiseled killing machine for the Military Industrial Complex, sent back into Vietnam to fix the historical results of the conflict in a brisk ninety minutes.

The decade of the '80s was filled with movies correcting mistakes of the past, both in front of and behind *First Blood Part II* on the calendar. Stallone saved POWs left behind in Vietnam, and Bruce Lee protégé Chuck Norris became Jim Braddock, a captured soldier who wasn't going to wait around to be saved in the *Missing in Action* films. Russian invaders were thwarted in *Red Dawn* by a scrappy bunch of white, Middle American do-gooders. And speaking of Russia, it was Stallone's Rocky Balboa who managed to go to the U.S.S.R. and end the Cold War in an impassioned speech about change following his not-so-surprising defeat of Ivan Drago in 1985's *Rocky IV*.

The expanse of action filmmaking was bigger and broader than ever in the '80s; it was all about the stars and the summer. This was the cinematic peak of Arnold Schwarzenegger—who, not to mention, took care of that pesky Columbian drug problem while rescuing his young daughter in 1985's *Commando*—Sylvester Stallone, Chuck Norris, and a whole slew of hopefuls with great athleticism, or a background in karate, or biceps as big as their heads. Acting was often secondary, as was directing.

The directors responsible for creating the new '80s action tidal wave did their job, make no mistake, and they produced some genre classics. They allowed the lens to capture every flex, every quip, every cinematic testosterone injection, and they made sure all the one-liners were crystal clear. They delivered the product, and fans gobbled it up faster than their popcorn.

But something was absent, even though nobody seemed to realize it at the time. Box-office returns for action films were through the roof, but style, substance, and depth were, for the most part, absent. The genre became an assembly line of explosions and mindless kinetics in place of any compelling storytelling. Mark Lester was the most prolific of the group, but he was inconsistent and never had the same success after *Commando*. George P. Cosmatos directed the second *Rambo* film, and he delivered the goods with 1993's Wyatt Earp actioner *Tombstone*. But he was also responsible for one of Sylvester Stallone's worst films, *Cobra*, and only directed ten feature films before his death in 2005.

Chuck Norris worked with filmmakers like Joseph Zito (*Missing in Action*), Lance Hool (*Braddock: Missing in Action 2*), and Menahem Golan (*The Delta Force*), mercenary directors who bounced from job to job, from genre to genre, producing products without any discernable personality.

When it came to straight action—wall-to-wall macho flex machines heavy on stunts and anemic in the plot department—there was no standout director to give these movies any clear leader. The finished products lacked identity and the quality suffered. The much-debated *auteur* theory, typically exclusive of genre filmmaking, had nevertheless found its way into horror via John Carpenter, George Romero, and Wes Craven by the late '80s.[2] But this sort of immediately identifiable directing talent was nonexistent in action movies, rendering the genre rudderless.

The stars were still there, however. By the time the late '80s rolled around, audiences still devoured anything and everything Arnold Schwarzenegger, the over-confident ruler of all things righteous. He had made his name as a cyborg villain in James Cameron's *The Terminator*, and he was America's hero, graciously adopted from Austria. His blustering braggadocio was a perfect fit for the temperament of a country embracing the capitalist zeitgeist. Bullets went out of their way to miss Schwarzenegger as he wiped the streets clean of crooked gangsters or saved his young daughter, or sought revenge on those who enslaved him as a youth as he did in his first big hit, *Conan the Barbarian*. But in 1986, Schwarzenegger had his most disappointing movie of the decade, *Raw Deal*, a film that was roundly denounced by critics. That same year, Schwarzenegger's big rival, Sylvester Stallone, had a critically derided film himself in *Cobra*. Both of these films doubled their budget at the box office, but they were, for lack of a better term, just plain bad movies. It was a sign that the action genre needed a change.

Times and moods were also changing again in America and across the world. Nothing lasts forever, especially not the idea of an action hero so succinctly attached to the American ideological pendulum, which started swinging in the opposite direction after the overindulgence of the decade began to wane. Then, in 1987, audiences were introduced to the defining buddy-cop action film with Shane Black's *Lethal Weapon* (five years after the buddy-cop subgenre made some noise with *48 Hrs.*), which showed studios there could be more to high-adrenaline spectacles than

Introduction

mercenary filmmaking.³ But where *Lethal Weapon* forged a fresh trail in the genre, it was the direction of John McTiernan that eventually signaled an overarching sea change, legitimizing the action genre as a place where fresh creative geniuses could make their mark. His early films would put a defining stamp on action, drawing critical acclaim and big box-office numbers, launching franchises, and in one case, birthing so many imitators that they became their own subgenre.

McTiernan brought distinct directorial vision to action cinema that had been mostly absent (even in the hands of *Lethal Weapon*'s Richard Donner, whose style and thematic storytelling took a backseat to the serendipitous teaming of Mel Gibson and Danny Glover), somehow managing to sneak that *auteur* theory into "guy movies." His European tutelage, and the way he worked this influence into the films he made with subtle editing and camera tricks both old and new, were just some of the ways McTiernan became the catalyst for a new wave of smart action movies with a pulse and a soul. Like James Cameron in sci-fi before him, John McTiernan's films were definitively *his* works. But unlike Cameron, McTiernan's action films steered clear of the stratospheric epic setting, shrinking the scope in support of the characters traversing his dangerous situations. Even in his broadest and most audacious storylines—of which he had his fair share—in the better ones it was intimacy and humanity that remained the driving force; these human elements proved to be the missing ingredient.

Beyond his technique, McTiernan's early films broke down barriers between the audience and the star. Not only had there been the ever-present fourth wall in '80s action, but what seemed like a fifth one, with audiences gazing upon these men—seemingly immortal men—performing impossible feats with ease. Otherworldly saviors, the superhero without spandex. The size of these men on the silver screen almost felt proportionate to who they were in real life. They were invincible giants, righting wrongs. The viewer was separated, miles apart from these action stars as they sat in the safety of a darkened theater, watching men with physicality they would most likely never see in the real world, vanquishing foes with ease. It worked for a while, but as audiences searched for someone with whom they could identify, they were coming up empty-handed.

McTiernan changed all of this with characters who were not supreme rulers or some sort of unbreakable pop Adonis. Even when they would pose as macho tough guys, his heroes were shot, killed, beaten down, filled with doubt and the very real human emotions of fear and apprehension.

Introduction

They used their brains more often than their brawn, because their brawn could fail them. He added a third dimension to characters that were, in the '80s, flat gun-toting pinballs personified. This cultivated a newfangled era of the genre, where the heroes saving the day felt like actual humans with whom audiences could genuinely connect.

Action movies would never be the same.

It began early, when McTiernan made a name for himself in the jungle. It solidified in 1988, when he introduced the world to John McClane, and it carried on through his other early films as the calendar ushered in a new decade and a new direction. In the span of three years, John McTiernan ascended to the top of the genre's mountain, building a portfolio of guy movies with one foot on the ground, where flaws and brains superseded infallibility and arrogance. And then, from those early days into the second act of his career, ambition and scope occasionally got the better of him as he began pushing back against the (often misguided) studio system. The subtlety with which he changed the face of an entire genre early on became no longer a quiet grassroots movement, but direct parody in his work in 1993. It was a misstep, and it wouldn't be the last time a movie got away from him. The studio system would, more than once, sabotage McTiernan's better intentions.

But John McTiernan, forever resilient and dogged, a focused artist with a mechanical approach to his craft, would bounce back. He also managed to pull off a phenomenal little magic trick in the late '90s, remaking a film and doing something almost impossible in the process: creating what is a better version of the original in every measurable way.

And then, just as quickly as things were up, they were down. Again.

McTiernan allowed the cynicism of Hollywood and his own professional paranoia to pollute both his filmmaking and his general views of the system. Decisions would undo his personal life in one of the most bizarre celebrity scandals of the twenty-first century, and everything would come crashing down.

Because Nothing Lasts Forever.

There is still time for John McTiernan to retrench, to recapture the energy and inventiveness he so expertly built in his early days. It will be a tough road with very few bridges to re-cross after his tumultuous fall from grace. But no matter what the future of action filmmaking has in store for John McTiernan, the past would never have been what it was without him.

Part I

Euros and Nomads

1

The European Influence

There was never going to be another path for John Campbell McTiernan, Jr., no matter how many other interests may have had his attention through his formative years.

Born January 8, 1951, in Albany, New York, John is the son of John Sr. and Myra McTiernan. John Sr. lost his sight in World War II, though it did not stop him from becoming a successful attorney when he returned to the United States. And his blindness pragmatically directed him to the world of music. He was an obsessive lover of classical music and opera, even performing arias himself at festivals, to which he would often bring John Jr.

He would also take young John along when he interviewed clients and various people for his law practice. After they would leave these interviews, John Sr. would ask his son what the person's face looked like when they said a certain thing. It was helpful for the blind litigator, but little did he know it would be a helpful tool for his son down the road, when John Jr. would begin immersing himself in foreign films.

These kinds of early influences would shape John's desires and his ultimate approach to filmmaking. But when John Jr. was an early adolescent, his father fell ill with a rare tropical virus he had contracted while on an opera tour in, of all places, Maine. This forced John Jr., his mother, and his sister to move back to a farm in upstate New York and live with Myra's parents while his father recovered. While there, John attended Phillips Exeter, a New Hampshire prep school. And like many of the greats, a teenaged John McTiernan didn't quite fit in with those around him. Phillips Exeter was, and is, a preparatory school with a rich history of Latin-scripted crests and Old World tradition; a common New England institution, and a place where the pastoral sensibilities of John McTiernan were too outside the status quo for his peers to accept. Without much of a social life in school, he retreated into the local cinemas. Like Scorsese and De Palma before him, he dedicated most of his free time to seeing and experiencing as many films as he could in his youth.

McTiernan fell so deeply in love with the movies that he almost passed on a chance to attend Juilliard to study theater directing—his first passion and the place he felt would best satiate his creative desires—in lieu of filmmaking. But despite his newfound adoration of the silver screen, McTiernan knew the possibility was too good to pass up.

He did go to Juilliard for a time, and along the way he worked on a few plays. He picked up some valuable lessons regarding the mechanics of directing and working with a cast, a trait that would come in handy with expansive casts, sets, and expectations. But, ultimately, McTiernan saw stage directing as a hobby for the rich, a career to which he never truly aspired.

Roughly halfway through his collegiate career, he transferred from Juilliard to the State University of New York, where his interest in cinema was fully ignited. The university was experimenting with a new film program, and McTiernan was only one of a handful of students who weren't spending their free time smoking marijuana. His diligence allowed him to use the university funding and equipment without much competition, and with this freedom he produced two short films in the program, an adaptation of *Poor Richard's Almanack* and a short called *Meditation.*

After graduating from SUNY, in 1974, McTiernan directed a movie which lies somewhere between a short film and a feature: *The Demon's Daughter.* He filmed the extremely low-budget Viking adventure in the woods outside his grandparents' farm where he'd grown up, performing the small tricks of an eager young director, like pasting hairpieces atop ponies to make them look like Viking steeds. He managed to get *The Demon's Daughter* done for $10,000, but he knew he needed to improve his approach to filmmaking and raise some funds for his next movie to get any graduate program to notice his work. McTiernan and his girlfriend at the time, Carol Land, raised enough capital to direct *Tales of the 22nd Century*, a feature-length film that was good enough to get him accepted into the graduate program at the American Film Institute in Los Angeles. So, in his early twenties, McTiernan said goodbye to his family and friends, packed up, and moved out to Southern California with Land, whom he would marry on October 12, 1974.

1. The European Influence

The American Film Institute, with alumni like Terrence Malick, Martin Brest, David Lynch, Darren Aronofsky, and Patty Jenkins, opened John McTiernan's world. He fell in love with the structure and craftsmanship of filmmaking, he began to understand new and inventive ways to tell his stories, and he looked to the French New Wave to further fortify his motivations.

There was no immediate film or singular moment that spoke to McTiernan, some magical turning point reaching out to touch him in an otherwise empty theater balcony and stir his creative soul. No, it came like most things in McTiernan's life, with a calculated decision to focus on filmmaking first. At the AFI he learned how to take movies apart and put them back together to see how the pieces fit. It's a technique he would come to call "reverse engineering" on the medium. He sought to learn what a movie *was*, not relying solely on his emotional experiences to define his understanding.

The classes at the AFI did not use a traditional grading system for its students, which fit McTiernan's sensibilities. He was never a poor student, but letter grades were secondary to what he knew he could do behind a camera. He had little time for textbooks. The only academic award the school handed out was similar to a "Most Likely to Succeed" accolade every year. The winner of the award would then be an intern to the resident filmmaker. For McTiernan, who won the award, it was Czech filmmaker Ján Kadár. Here was, again, a European filmmaker from whom he could learn, and a director who would become the most powerful influence in McTiernan's understanding of the art on its basest of levels.

Born in April of 1918 in Czechoslovakia, Jewish-Slovak filmmaker Ján Kadár endured the labor camps during World War II before he was able to turn his love of photography into a filmmaking career once the war ended and the Czechoslovakian state became a socialist republic ally of the Soviet Union. He broke into the industry with a pair of short documentaries about Slovakia rebuilding after the war, and from there he would soon become the face of the Czech New Wave.

Kadár's 1965 film *Obchod na korze* (*The Shop on Main Street*) was his eighth feature film but the first work in his expansive career—and in the Czech filmmaking industry as a whole—to find international praise. Taking place during World War II, the film tells the story of Tono (Jozef Kroner), a man who befriends an elderly Jewish woman in the days before the Jewish community in Czechoslovakia was rounded up and taken away by Nazi forces. *The Shop on Main Street* won the Academy Award for Best Foreign Language Film in 1965, and the success convinced Kadár to try his hand at Hollywood only a few years later.

While in Hollywood he directed the relatively overlooked feature *The Angel Levine* in 1970, but spent most of his American career directing movies for television. In 1975 he directed the critically acclaimed drama *Lies My Father Told Me*, about a Jewish boy's upbringing in Montreal. Around that same time he worked as the resident filmmaker at the AFI, where he met his eager young assistant John McTiernan.

Kadár's philosophy was to approach a film like composers tackle a piece of music. He would tell McTiernan not to look at a movie as a film necessarily, but as a piece of music, or a concerto. This approach allows the viewer to find the proper key, where the movements in the story occur, and the rhythm of the picture becomes clear. To Kadár, there are notes to a film just as there are frames. This sort of analytical approach to filmmaking was the perfect combination of McTiernan's father's musical background and John Jr.'s own desire to break apart a film to see how it works.

Kadár would also instruct his young protégé to memorize the movies. Not the plot, that was the easy part, but each and every shot of the film. If pressed, he should be able to visually lay out a film with his eyes closed. The director would assign McTiernan several complicated films of the French New Wave, stories with moving cuts and dream sequences and whatever else the director had in mind, and he would tell McTiernan to study it. Kadár informed his new pupil that he must live inside a world of pictures to fully understand the way they are supposed to work.

And so McTiernan would dissect films shot for shot, frame by frame, and this technique would help him work from the outside in, then back out again. The film with which he finally perfected this technique was François Truffaut's *Day for Night* (1973). He watched it for three consecutive days, hours upon end each day, until he was able to see through the film on the screen. His technical deconstruction of the movie, at least from the viewer's experience, allowed him to almost see things from the other side of the lens, to understand why directors do certain things and when they decide to reach into their bag of tricks. His technical mastery learned at the AFI was now working for him, helping understand Truffaut's filmmaking with the precision of a surgeon.

Day for Night is similar to Federico Fellini's semi-autobiographical film *8½*, in that they both involve a director flailing about while trying to

1. The European Influence

get their career back on track.[1] In Truffaut's film it is he who plays the director, Ferrand, a man struggling to get his melodrama *Je Vous Présente Paméla* (*Meet Pamela*) off the ground.[2] The star of the hokey picture within the picture is Jean-Pierre Aumont's Alexandre, an aging star barely hanging on to relevance. Valentina Cortese is his co-star, and a young Jacqueline Bisset plays a woman recovering from a nervous breakdown. These stars and the minutiae of everyday life on the set are what keep *Day for Night* churning along. That, and the romantic trysts of the cast and crew behind the scenes. It would go on to win Best Foreign Language Film at the Academy Awards ceremony, and the BAFTA Award for Best Film in 1974, right about the time John McTiernan was taking it apart and putting it back together.

Something else McTiernan did while watching *Day for Night* was to ignore the dialogue subtitles. It was something he'd gotten used to. Hearkening back to the earlier attorney-client interview sessions with his blind father, McTiernan honed in on the characters' expressions rather than their words. His attention was not on what the people in the scene were saying in this foreign language, but how they were saying it and what they looked like while doing so. That way, he could study the more dramatic side of filmmaking while still using the rigid deconstructionist approach.

The meta-fictional structure of *Day for Night* also stuck with McTiernan; at least it seemed to later in his career when he would embark on his own sort of meta-fictional satire of the film industry. Unfortunately, his venture was upended and sabotaged and manipulated to the point where it resembled *Meet Pamela*, the flimsy picture in *Day for Night*, more than Truffaut's film.

The French New Wave, which was already heavily influencing the sensibilities of 1970s New Hollywood movement, would become McTiernan's central motivating era of filmmaking while at the AFI. Truffaut's eccentricities, in a film about the making a film, was McTiernan's first conscious deconstruction of a picture, and that sort of technical prowess, coupled with the neo-realism and idiosyncratic camerawork in European cinema at the time, subconsciously created a through-line for his own career.

A unique vision was shaping in John McTiernan's approach to filmmaking. Raised in a somewhat traditional American "rural" lifestyle, educated in quality schools, influenced by European filmmakers, and obsessed with the technical workings of the craft, McTiernan's work as a director would eventually reflect the balance of his life in a grounded personal style with the ability to handle epic casts and epic scope. But success would not appear for a little while, as McTiernan would spend the better part of the next decade directing commercials to pay the bills. In the summer of 1981, after graduating from the AFI Conservatory, McTiernan began crafting a supernatural screenplay.

In 1985, the same year his first daughter, Isabella, was born, McTiernan was finally given the opportunity to direct his first studio feature film, *Nomads*, the aforementioned supernatural thriller he had been writing since graduating from the AFI.[3] A small production company, headed by Elliott Castner, purchased the screenplay and gave him a scant budget to put the film together. It was an inauspicious beginning. But the right people would set their sights on it and see what McTiernan had to offer behind the clumsiness of a first-time filmmaker.

2

Nomads

The less said about *Nomads*, the better. It was the jumping-off point for McTiernan, and there is no question that the film was a terrific project for him on which to sharpen his tools. But the problem with this trial-and-error approach becomes clear in the finished product. There were little to no expectations of the film, purchased by an unknown production company called Atlantic Releasing Company (ARC), and very few people saw it.[1] *Nomad*s was John McTiernan's own version of *Boxcar Bertha*; it was nothing more than learning on the fly.[2] Whatever happened in the end, he was given a budget of $1 million, well over ten times the budget of any of his student films, so he was happy and eager to get going.

And from then on, for better or for worse, John McTiernan was a legitimate director.

Originally, the role of French anthropologist Charles Pommier in *Nomads* belonged to French thespian Gerard Depardieu, an actor who had yet to make any mark in the United States. Except ARC needed a name recognizable to American audiences to play the lead, though they couldn't get anywhere near the A-list talent of the time with a flimsy, low-budget genre picture like *Nomads*. They could, however, land a burgeoning TV star, someone who was just beginning to make a name for himself as a decent actor on a moderately successful series. Someone like Pierce Brosnan.

The Irish-born Brosnan had been a television actor since 1980, save for a small but brilliant role in John Mackenzie's *The Long Good Friday* that same year. And by 1986, his action-comedy television series *Remington Steele* had become a solid hit for NBC. Brosnan was excited to play the tortured French anthropologist of *Nomads*, the polar opposite of his suave James Bond–esque character in *Remington Steele*. (Ironic, since Brosnan would take on the Bond role in 1995's *Goldeneye,* and subsequently build an impressive cache of *Remington Steele*–type characters throughout his career. This Included a project he would take on with McTiernan in the late '90s.)

Having Brosnan on board was a big positive for McTiernan and the movie; people wanted to see if Remington Steele could carry a major motion picture, so it built at least a little intrigue. Production was relatively smooth. McTiernan secured legendary composer Bill Conti to write the score. And then, while shooting one of the scenes at Brosnan's home, an explosion of gunfire erupted down the street.³ Production shut down and a quick investigation revealed that Tony Scott was filming a climactic gun battle scene for *Beverly Hills Cop II*. The noise was intrusive, but McTiernan and his team lacked the sort of pull to ask Tony Scott, Jerry Bruckheimer, and Don Simpson to pause their massive production so he could secure a few shots for his $1 million movie.

Instead, the cast and crew rehearsed through the gunfire and stayed alert for breaks and resets. If anything, it added a little perspective for McTiernan. He still had some work to do to get to the point where he held sway in Hollywood; before long it would be his own production forcing smaller films to wait until *he* was finished. The moment also spoke to the breadth of each movie's production; *Beverly Hills Cop II* didn't open until May 20, 1987, where *Nomads* was wrapped, edited, and pushed into theaters on March 7, 1986.

There is an interesting tale to be told somewhere inside the mess that is *Nomads*, a convoluted story about ancient Eskimo witchcraft, urban gangs, a mad anthropologist, and a young doctor desperate for answers. It's all here, tied up in a disheveled collage of blurry pulp storytelling and confusing transitions.

Leslie-Anne Down is Dr. Eileen Flax, an ER doctor who has the misfortune of being at work the night Jean Charles Pommier (Brosnan) is brought in, bloody, ranting and raving in his native French tongue. While Eileen is examining Jean, he springs up from his bed, bites her ear, and whispers something to her: "N'y sont pas; sont des Inuit." ("They are not there; they are Inuit.")

These words somehow transfer all of Pommier's memories into Eileen, and the story propels forward from there into a mishmash of muddled visuals and an oddly minimal amount of dialogue. It's incredibly confusing, and this is where McTiernan seems to lose a grip on his camera's ability to tell the story. Points of view shift as Eileen's memories become

Pommier's. We find out that Pommier is a French anthropologist who just recently moved to Los Angeles with his wife. Almost immediately, a neighborhood band of punk-rock misfits spray-paint words on his garage door. Through all the mire is the introduction of the aforementioned Inuit Eskimos, demonic muckrakers who have possessed Pommier. It is all executed with such disregard for scenes to come before and after it, and wordless stretches when dialogue would help explain what is happening.

Nomads plods along through tedious scenes where it generally feels like, with the advantage of hindsight regarding what was right around the corner in McTiernan's career, he really is just trying some things out with the camera. There are no memorable shots or sequences, only a standard thriller aesthetic. The camera moves very little, even when movement feels necessary, and scenes go on too long without developing into anything of substance. A handful of scenes, intended to be tense, worked; many others did not. It's a surprising thing to see from McTiernan, who would master tension and economy of scenes over his next three pictures.

The final shot of *Nomads* reveals a twist regarding Brosnan's character, but by that time one of two things has happened ... or perhaps a little bit of both. Either the audience has stopped caring altogether, or they're so confused by the story that this twist at the California/Nevada border means pretty much nothing to them. Trying to engage with *Nomads* is a chore in so many ways because it commits the cardinal sin of bad movies: it's boring.

If anything can be said in praise of *Nomads*, it's the fact that McTiernan clearly got the best he could out of the actors. Pierce Brosnan, who would work with McTiernan again, dedicates himself to the role, despite his unfortunate French accent. Leslie-Anne Down is fine, respectable, and the rest of the cast does their job competently. The problems with the film lie in the cluttered execution. Sometimes, it happens to the very best directors in their early work.

Nomads disappeared almost as quickly as it arrived, a mere blip on the 1986 cinematic landscape when it was released on March 7, alongside *Highlander* and a *Care Bears* sequel. The film was a shapeless mess that felt bloated (despite clocking in at a mere ninety minutes) for audiences and critics alike, overwrought and flat. To this day, the box-office total for *Nomads* sits at just under $2.3 million; to put that in 2017 numbers—just to add some staggering perspective—that amount adjusted for inflation is still only $5.3 million.[4]

Critics were even less kind to the film, though some may have spotted a keen eye behind the camera showing flashes of confidence, simply lost in the wrong film. Part of the problem overall was the constantly shifting point of view. Roger Ebert said in his one-and-a-half star review, "Sometimes we see down and then we get a point-of-view shot that is supposed to be inside her [Leslie-Anne Down's character's] head but looking out through Brosnan's eyes. Sometimes we see Brosnan from the outside. Sometimes that means we are looking at the real Brosnan, and sometimes it doesn't. We'd really be confused, if we gave a damn."[5]

Perhaps *Nomads* can be dismissed as McTiernan trying to find what worked and what didn't. Some critics squinted, and noticed the slimmest of silver linings. Most decided to move on to the next slate of releases.

Regardless of its slight impact and critical derision, *Nomads* managed to catch the attention of the right superstar in Hollywood, one who knew John McTiernan had greatness in him.

Part II

Welcome to the Jungle

3
Predator

Jim Thomas had absolutely no inroads to Hollywood when he thought up the idea for his screenplay "Hunter."[1] Initially, it was about an alien hunter coming to Earth and stalking various large game, including humans, in different locations across the globe. But after some brainstorming sessions with his brother John, they pared the story down to a single alien, and a single group of humans. They decided on a platoon of super soldiers to make it as plausible as possible, and they changed the name from "Hunter" to "Predator."

Even if this initial draft of *Predator* had been perfect, the Thomas brothers had no way to get it into the right hands outside of the old-fashioned technique of mailing letters to studios, agents, producers—*anyone* they thought could get the script in front of someone who would be interested in purchasing their work. The rejections were fast and furious, and seemingly never ending, until they managed to get it in the door at 20th Century–Fox and the studio's new regime, spearheaded by Lawrence Gordon.

By the mid–1980s, there was arguably no producer in Hollywood as prolific and consistently reliable as Lawrence Gordon. The Mississippi native had been in Southern California since the late '60s, when he got his start under the tutelage of Aaron Spelling and his television production company, Four Star Television. Eventually he found his way to Columbia Pictures' TV division, Screen Gems, where he played a hand in assembling one of the most revered of all television movies, the 1971 football drama *Brian's Song*.

It was just the beginning for Gordon, who would soon team up with a tenacious action filmmaker named Walter Hill and produce Hill's greatest run of work: the Charles Bronson/James Coburn street-fight drama

Hard Times, the L.A. crime thriller *The Driver* starring Ryan O'Neal, the cult classic *The Warriors*, *48 Hrs.* in 1982, the underrated crime thriller *Streets of Fire* in 1984, and the rare Walter Hill comedy *Brewster's Millions* in 1985.

In 1984, Gordon became the president and chief operating officer for 20th Century–Fox, and it wasn't long after that when he was handed Jim and John Thomas's screenplay for *Predator*. He saw merit in it almost immediately, and after so many rejections and denials, the Thomas brothers had finally shoved their tattered screenplay in front of the eyes of the right producer.

Not many people saw *Nomads*. One person did, however; that is certain. And what he saw beneath all the messy production values and missteps was potential. That one person was Arnold Schwarzenegger, who was on board as the star of *Predator*. The biggest star in Hollywood in 1986, Schwarzenegger was working with Larry Gordon to get a director in place for his latest project; it was Schwarzenegger and his friend, producer John Davis, who had John McTiernan in mind.

Schwarzenegger saw *Nomads* and pointed it out to Gordon and his team. Even though the tension throughout the movie doesn't hold up, at the time Arnold was impressed with the ability for McTiernan to maintain whatever tension he could for such a no-budget feature. Above all else, Schwarzenegger wanted *Predator* to be suspenseful from the very beginning, before the action even kicked in. Schwarzenegger knew McTiernan was talented enough to handle his new film, so he and Davis talked Gordon and his producing partner, Joel Silver, into bringing in McTiernan to direct the film.[2]

Joel Silver had made his mark on Hollywood by the time 1986 rolled around. Teaming up with Lawrence Gordon Productions and becoming the head of the motion picture division, Silver splashed onto the Hollywood scene in 1979, working with Gordon to produce *The Warriors*. He'd also played a major part alongside Gordon in birthing the buddy-cop action formula and making Eddie Murphy a legitimate movie star with *48 Hrs.* (and later, in 1987, perfected said formula with Richard Donner's *Lethal Weapon*); Silver also helped define Arnold Schwarzenegger as *the* Hollywood action megastar—not just a flash in the pan—with *Commando* in 1985. By the time he and McTiernan crossed paths in the early days of *Predator* production, Silver had already built a reputation as somewhat of a tyrannical producer with an ego as supercharged as the movies he was producing. He lived large and he worked even larger, butting heads time and time again with several of the players in this, the late '80s Hollywood action renaissance, and building a reputation as a sometimes abusive, sometimes untrustworthy megalomaniac.

Silver became such a caricature of Hollywood id run amok, in fact, that he was parodied in Tony Scott's 1993 film *True Romance*. Scott—with an assist from screenwriter Quentin Tarantino—modeled Saul Rubinek's cocaine-addled yuppie super producer Lee Donowitz after Silver.

Predator was a big project for Fox, and it would kickstart McTiernan's career in every conceivable way. Nobody had seen or cared much about *Nomads*, true, but from the ashes of that film came his opportunity to get a foothold. Schwarzenegger was already attached as the star, anxious for a hit after the *Raw Deal* misstep, but McTiernan worked directly with Silver to have specific actors in supporting roles. And every one of them paid off.

Carl Weathers proved to be McTiernan's most crucial casting decision. A one-time San Diego State linebacker and Oakland Raider, Weathers left football behind in 1974 to pursue a career as an actor. It was clear, shortly thereafter, that the decision was wise. After a string of TV cameos

Arnold Schwarzenegger and John McTiernan taking a break on the set of *Predator* (20th Century–Fox, 1987).

and bit parts in movies, Weathers landed the role of Apollo Creed in the 1976 Best Picture winner, *Rocky*. Creed would become an iconic American character, one he would reprise three more times, through 1985's *Rocky IV*.

McTiernan understood Weathers' ability to "act," to perform with sincerity and truth, and he wanted someone to motivate Schwarzenegger into more honest acting. For all his successes, Arnold Schwarzenegger had never been pushed to tap into the more emotional side of his performances. McTiernan knew Schwarzenegger was still raw as an actor, and he appreciated Weathers' work in the *Rocky* films and his ability to bring out the best in Stallone. Weathers, in McTiernan's mind, would push and pull with Arnold not as a supporting player, but as an equal. And besides, he was more than physically adequate enough to square off against Arnold.[3]

Carl Weathers is an excellent adversary to Schwarzenegger and the entire platoon, a conniving outlier who only has the back of the other men because of the obligations of duty. He adds a tangential layer to the dynamic of the group, and he functions like a more active, interesting version of Paul Reiser's bumbling conman in *Aliens*.

McTiernan cast Shane Black as Hawkins, mostly to have another writer on set to bounce ideas off from time to time. Black was one of the fresh faces of action cinema in 1987, having just produced the whip-smart screenplay for *Lethal Weapon*, one of the biggest hits of the year.[4] Not only had it made megastars out of Mel Gibson and Danny Glover, but it made Black a hot screenwriting commodity. Black had an ability to create a fully realized world in his dialogue, heavy with macho posturing, aggression, and idiosyncratic humor. Jim and John Thomas were primarily responsible for the *Predator* screenplay, but the two "pussy" jokes the Hawkins character throws out in the film, arguably two of the screenplay's biggest highlights, were Black's idea.

The rest of the cast was filled up and out, and each of the central players decorated the periphery with great color and plenty of genuine craziness. Sonny Landham was Billy, the mystic mercenary who knows something is amiss very early on. Landham had landed bit parts in the '80s, including snippets in Walter Hill's *The Warriors*, and Tobe Hooper's *Poltergeist* before Hill cast him in a larger role in *48 Hrs*. It was that role that caught Silver's attention, and he brought Sonny Landham to McTiernan.

Landham was a bit of a loose cannon. Before starring in mainstream studio films he was an army veteran turned porn star in San Fernando Valley in the 1970s, the heyday of the industry. He had a short fuse and a more honest edge to him than any of the chiseled stars in the film pretending to play tough guys. But he was also a violent man, even when unprovoked. In fact, Landham needed a personal bodyguard, not to keep people from attacking him, but to prevent him from going after other members of the cast; the studio would not insure Landham's hiring without it.

And then there was Jesse Ventura, a pro wrestler then at the peak of his career, cast in the film at Schwarzenegger's recommendation. Ventura, formerly Jesse Janos, was himself a navy veteran and member of the underwater demolition unit. He served in Vietnam, but saw no combat in the South Pacific. After leaving the navy, Ventura joined a motorcycle club in Southern California before becoming a bodybuilder and, later, a wrestler.

His alter ego in the wrestling world was Jesse "The Body," and he officially changed his last name to Ventura to go with his Venice Beach bodybuilder persona. For several years in the early '80s, Ventura built a successful career and became one of the stars of the sport, shouting threats through spittle and leaning into his boastful creation, until blood clots were discovered in his lungs. These, he claimed, were from his exposure to Agent Orange in Vietnam. The condition put an end to his career in the ring.

In retirement, after a handful of failed returns, Ventura became a personality outside the ring, and an ambassador for the sport. He hosted a wrestling show, did color commentary on matches, and, in 1986, found himself cast as Blain, a wheel-gun wielding, tobacco-chewing tough guy in a sea of tough guys, in *Predator*.[5]

Bill Duke, a six-foot-four-inch African American actor who had arguably the most diverse acting background of the platoon, was cast as Mac, Blain's closest friend. Duke had starred in the 1976 blaxploitation classic *Car Wash*, and in Paul Schrader's moody thriller *American Gigolo* as a gay pimp. Once the action renaissance began to take shape in the mid–'80s, Duke found a reliable new road in his career. He was cast opposite Arnold Schwarzenegger in *Commando*, and the two built a strong friendship during that shoot. It was Schwarzenegger, once again, suggesting a friend for a role and having the suggestion pay off.

Character actor Richard Chaves filled out the platoon as Poncho, the least influential member of the group but the last victim of the Predator.

Veteran Mexican actress Elpidia Carrillo was cast as Anna, a prisoner the platoon takes with them after the initial assault on the guerrilla base.

The human cast was complete, and production was underway. But McTiernan still needed to figure out the most effective way to present the title character, the Predator. As production began in late April of 1986, this would prove to be the biggest obstacle of the entire shoot.

4

The Van Damme Experiment

Early concept art of the Predator character was all over the map. McTiernan and his production designer John Vallone submitted an initial rendering of the alien that was spindly and spider-like, which was resoundingly rejected. They went back to the drawing board and came up with a large, horned beast with a strange sort of duck-billed concoction serving as a mouth. It was frustrating McTiernan and Vallone, trying to find the right mixture of practicality and menace in their Predator. But the shooting schedule waits for no director, so McTiernan and his crew pushed forward. Besides, a great majority of the early action would feature a stunt man in a red leotard standing in as the shape of the creature, and it would be keyed out and replaced with an effect that would indicate the Predator's ability to bend light and seem invisible. The monster didn't show up until the third act, when he would face off with Schwarzenegger. Since McTiernan preferred to shoot in sequence as much as he could in order for his actors to get an honest feel for their characters and motivations in any given scene, they had time to figure that out.

For the early invisibility scenes, McTiernan hired an unknown Belgian actor named Jean-Claude Van Damme to slip into the red suit. From there, the headaches began.

Jean-Claude Van Damme, born October 18, 1960, began his martial arts training at the age of ten, and he was competing in professional tournaments by the time he was twelve. He became a professional kickboxer in 1977, and accumulated a gaudy 18–1 record from 1977 to 1982. Then, in 1982, he moved to Hollywood with stars in his eyes. He grabbed bit roles in *Breakin'* and *Missing in Action* in 1984 before playing the villain in the 1986 martial arts film *No Retreat, No Surrender*. And then, 20th Century–Fox and John McTiernan came calling.

Part II: Welcome to the Jungle

Van Damme had befriended casting director Jackie Burch during his short time in Hollywood, and was constantly hassling her for work. He was especially proud of his ability as an athlete, and would perform impressive roundhouse kicks in Burch's office over and over in the hopes this would help him land a plum role. When Burch was hired to fill out the cast of *Predator*, she suggested Van Damme because of his agility, as well as his tenacity.

Like any young, eager action star, Jean-Claude Van Damme jumped at the chance to play any kind of part in a motion picture as big-time as *Predator*; even if he did have to wear what he thought at the time was going to be just a little makeup once the final alien costume was complete.[1] And, like so many European young men with the desire to make it in Hollywood, the chance to work alongside someone like Arnold Schwarzenegger, the shining example of what Tinseltown can do for a fellow Eastern-European immigrant, was an incredible bonus. It all sounded great, and the crew assured Van Damme that even though he would have to wear a leotard as the alien stalker he would still be able to run and jump and show off some of his martial arts work. The suit wouldn't get in his way.

But then they did a plaster cast of Van Damme for the suit, tailored the design to fit his physique, and started to realize that with all the machinations of the suit and all the things it would have to do just to move fluidly, there would be virtually no opportunity for Van Damme to perform any jumps or spin moves. Instead, he would have to lumber across the jungle setting. He was dejected, but he played the good solider—for a while, anyway.

It wasn't until Van Damme had put on the suit a few times and performed a handful of scenes that he realized his character was going to be invisible the majority of the time anyway. Not only would he be denied a chance to show off in front of Arnold Schwarzenegger, he wouldn't even be seen in the finished product, save for a few scenes in the end. And even then, when it was time for his character to make himself visible to Schwarzenegger, Van Damme would be wearing a creature suit that would again hide his entire body.

For weeks Van Damme shot these "invisible" scenes in the red predator suit, but all the while he was seething at the way things were going. McTiernan was beginning to clench a bit as well, checking the post daily to see if the suit for the predator had arrived. Eventually it did, and the ultimate reveal was discouraging, to say the least.

4. The Van Damme Experiment

This first creation of the Predator costume had that duck-billed mouth from the concept art, but it was also rather fragile and passive looking when McTiernan pried the nails from the crate and lifted the suit up into the air for everyone to see. It was scaly and weak and non-threatening in an almost comical way. McTiernan knew then that the creature creation would have to be re-imagined yet again. More delays, more money, more headaches. But despite his better judgment, McTiernan begrudgingly gave this costume a chance.

He tried out Van Damme in the suit, but it was a short-lived experiment. McTiernan could see the halt in production coming from a mile away. And he was right; after the studio executives saw the dailies with Van Damme lumbering around in the trees wearing this absurd costume, everything was put on hold until a proper villain could be created.

McTiernan knew who could solve this entire problem: Stan Winston. But hiring that legend of makeup would be more difficult than it sounded.

Stan Winston started his career in the fast-and-loose world of B horror movies and drive-in dreck. He would do makeup work for TV movies nobody remembers, with titles like *Gargoyles* or *Parasite*, and special-effects work for projects like *Manimal*, a 1983 TV series about a man who can change himself into any animal he wants and uses his power to fight crime. The ridiculousness of these stories was of no consequence for Winston; what was important was perfecting his makeup and effects work. In 1982, Winston filled in on the set of John Carpenter's *The Thing*, doing some of the creature work while Rob Bottin took time off to recharge his batteries.

Then, in 1984, he teamed up with James Cameron and Arnold Schwarzenegger to create a futuristic killer cyborg. This cyborg, the T-100, is sent back in time to kill the mother of the future leader of men; he would also be encased in human tissue—Schwarzenegger's human tissue—for a large portion of the film. The movie gave Winston a chance to flex his creative muscles.

The Terminator would become a turning point film for everyone involved. It made Schwarzenegger a star, Cameron one of the hottest new genre directors, and Winston the most desired special-effects man in the business.

Two years later, Winston and Cameron teamed up to expand on Ridley Scott and H. R. Giger's Xenomorph creation in the 1979 classic *Alien*. The sequel, entitled *Aliens*, would be an entirely different experience than

Part II: Welcome to the Jungle

the original film, a visceral and frenetic action-adventure instead of a moody atmospheric horror like the original. And the eponymous aliens would number in the hundreds—with a queen. These new innovations were the product of Winston who, once again, delivered some of the more iconic monsters in popular culture. *Aliens* was another monumental hit for Cameron and Winston, so when John McTiernan begged for him to come and fix the *Predator* issue, it required more money than the project had to offer.

Schwarzenegger initially brought up Winston when he realized things were going south. He'd talked to McTiernan about their collaboration on *The Terminator*, and McTiernan was convinced Winston could cure all that ailed. Only McTiernan had no sort of leverage during the *Predator* shoot to secure a single dollar beyond the budget. Larry Gordon, who'd been around the block in Hollywood by 1986, stepped up on McTiernan's behalf; Gordon had enough clout, and they got the money, and Stan Winston was brought on board to get the production back on its feet.

That was the last anyone saw of Jean-Claude Van Damme on set. It's uncertain whether he was fired or simply ignored until he went away. There are more than a handful of accounts of Van Damme's dismissal

Carl Weathers (left) and a dejected Jean-Claude Van Damme between takes on the *Predator* (20th Century–Fox, 1987) set.

4. The Van Damme Experiment

depending on who is speaking on the matter, but whatever the case, he was not going to be the ideal fit for what Winston had in mind anyway.

The main inspirations for the Predator creature came from two outside sources. The first was a painting in Joel Silver's office of an old Rastafarian warrior. It's what spurred Winston in the right direction, a realization that this alien creature needs to be physically imposing and large enough to prove a worthy adversary for a muscle-bound platoon of elite soldiers. It's also why the five-foot-ten-inch Van Damme was replaced with Kevin Peter Hall, a stuntman who stands seven-three.[2]

The second bit of motivation was crucial for the Predator's jowls. While Winston was frantically trying to put together an acceptable sketch of the alien hunter, he was also in the middle of the press circuit for *Aliens*, which had just been released and was a huge hit. He and James Cameron were on a flight to Japan for a symposium when Cameron flippantly mentioned mandibles as something he would like to see on a monster. Mandibles, or gills (like those on the creature from the Black Lagoon) would add a unique look to the Predator. Winston sketched the mandibles on the face of his Rastafarian warrior, and the creature was born.

But then came the struggle of how to realize this creation on screen. Digital effects were certainly an option, but the digital-effects industry was still in its infancy. CGI—in its modern definition—did not exist yet, and wouldn't really until James Cameron introduced his alien in 1989's *The Abyss*. The invisibility scenes would work with the technology of the time, but once the Predator loses its cloak the visible monster must look threatening. A computer-generated Predator would have a detached look, and it wouldn't be imposing enough up against the flesh-and-blood mass of Arnold Schwarzenegger.

Despite his initial desire to push the limits of special effects in 1986, Winston opted to stay practical. Having seven-foot-three actor Kevin Peter Hall in a suit with an elaborate mask and a unique tribal webbing across his body would make a great deal more sense in this case. It would add texture and weight to those final scenes with Schwarzenegger. McTiernan and the studio heads agreed with this assessment, and production was green lit once again.

5

A Survival Story

The villain had been figured out, but it wasn't going to be the only issue to plague the *Predator* shoot. As to be expected, a big-budget film involving a relatively green filmmaker, lavish jungle sets, and a whole host of makeup and special effects was an endurance test of the highest order. Aside from the failed Van Damme experiment, the cast and crew had to fight through all manner of technical issues, location inconsistencies, leeches, snakes, and given the limited access to clean food and water, the potential for dysentery.

In fact, just about everyone involved with the shoot came down with diarrhea at one point or another while filming in the jungles of Central Mexico. Everyone that is, except McTiernan and Arnold Schwarzenegger, both of whom refused to eat any of the local food or use any of the water in the hotel. McTiernan and Schwarzenegger each lost around twenty-five pounds during production.[1]

The first big logistical issue involved the jungle setting. McTiernan and Donald McAlpine had to beg Fox to allow them to shoot in an actual jungle rather than on sound stages. They were given the okay, but then they handed over the location to a scout who decided on Puerto Vallarta. What the scout never bothered to research was the foliage in West Central Mexico, which began shedding its leaves about the time production began. It made the floor of the "jungle" brown, the trees devoid of any leaves. What made things worse were the accompanying second-unit scenes filmed in Jalisco, where the foliage looked appropriately dense and colorful. It created continuity issues, but it was just something McTiernan would have to deal with. Only later did McTiernan realize the location scout responsible for picking Puerto Vallarta chose the area because he had rental properties in the city he wanted to work on during the shoot, with

5. A Survival Story

the help of a few extra crew members, no less. It was the last time McTiernan let anyone else pick a spot for his movie.

The only big props required for *Predator*, outside the guerrilla outpost set and the jungle itself, were three Huey helicopters to transport the platoon to and from the jungle. The arrival of Dutch and the other mercenaries also included—aside from the alien craft landing on Earth during the credits sequence that was added in post-production, the first digital effect of the movie—Schwarzenegger's cigar. They weren't allowed to light the cigar inside the chopper, so the flame was added after the fact.

McTiernan and his crew arrived in the jungle to find some three hundred union-hired Mexican workers waiting to be told what to do. McTiernan didn't have enough work for that many employees, and they caused logistical headaches and overcrowding on the jungle sets. Eventually, he sent home at least half of the union workers, all of whom were paid for their time.

The weather in Central Mexico was stiflingly humid, and the terrain was problematic; flat spaces among the trees were practically nonexistent, and snakes were everywhere. As Kevin Peter Hall, the Predator himself, put it in an interview on the Stan Winston School of Character Arts website, *Predator* "wasn't a film. It was an endurance test for all of us." He then cited a chase scene between he and Schwarzenegger through stagnant water full of leeches.[2]

With all this testosterone floating around the set, some strange macho competitions popped up from time to time. Ventura was pretty excited when he found out from the wardrobe department—at least he was convinced by wardrobe—that his biceps were one inch larger in diameter than Arnold Schwarzenegger's. He suggested a measuring contest, with the winner getting a bottle of champagne from the loser. What he didn't account for, however, was Schwarzenegger's ability to persuade. Behind the scenes, he convinced the wardrobe department to tell Ventura that Schwarzenegger's arms were bigger, and Ventura was on the hook for a bottle of bubbly.

Most of the actors would wake up at all hours of the early morning—some as early as three a.m.—to get in a workout before filming began that day to make sure their arms were nice and toned for the cameras. Carl Weathers, however, would make sure and do his workouts when nobody else was around because he liked telling everyone it was just his natural physique.

The assault on the guerrilla compound at the end of the first act was shot by a second unit, with McTiernan filming the aftermath. He didn't care for the work of second-unit director Craig R. Baxley, who filmed the set piece using static wide shots and little movement. A careful viewing of this scene shows that McTiernan was correct, as the action of the scene has a different aesthetic, but there was little he could do given the time and budget constraints.

Working chronologically through the film, the next roadblock came in the form of the Predator's thermal vision. McTiernan wanted to use an actual heat-vision camera to capture the point of view of the hunter. He secured one of these cameras, but it came with two issues. First, there was the issue of the machine itself being a cumbersome piece of equipment with a cord that would only extend a few feet from the van in which it was delivered. Second, and more importantly, the heat of the jungle was too great to differentiate from the actors' body temperatures. Trying to water down the trees in the background or have actors stand in front of fires proved futile exercises, and the whole approach was scrapped.

This was one of the first instances where McTiernan learned how to manipulate a production in his favor. Without seeking approval first, McTiernan hired a small production company to digitally create a "Predator Vision." Only after they were finished, and he was able to show off their impressive work, did he mention the fact that he had gone over budget to get it done. Thankfully, the effects were perfect, so the studio couldn't really argue.

Another small issue during the shoot involved the Predator's blood, which was originally orange. It didn't photograph properly, barely standing out against the jungle backdrop. One of the effects assistants suggested cutting open some of the glow sticks they had on set and using that for blood, and it worked beautifully.

The all-out machine-gun blitz in the jungle following Blain's murder, the one where Poncho informs the team at the end of the scene that they "hit nothing," was McTiernan's idea. He found the American audience's lust for artillery and gunfire fascinating, and wanted some way to "take the piss out" of guns and weapons in the movie.[3]

Even though the day shoots were incredibly hot and humid, the night scenes were freezing cold. And these were all scenes involving Schwarzenegger, who was covered in mud from head to toe, and Kevin Peter Hall, safely insulated in his Predator suit.[4] Schwarzenegger, perpetually cold

5. A Survival Story

and wet under a cake of jungle mud during the night scenes, would shiver uncontrollably between takes, so much so that the heat lamps on set did little to warm him up. He even tried drinking some schnapps, but that just made him inebriated. He would still be shivering cold, but at least he was relaxed.

The 20th Century–Fox studio wouldn't allow McTiernan to shoot in anamorphic widescreen, which he wanted to use to capture the expansive jungle landscapes. Executives claimed it was too expensive. So, in another recalcitrant move—even more telling of the rebellious spirit that would get him in trouble down the road—McTiernan used an anamorphic version of the studio logo to open the film, which made the 20th Century–Fox logo look stretched out and ill-fitting. It was a subtle thumbing of his nose to Fox, who didn't mind when the finished product hit theaters.

Predator was one of the ten highest-grossing films of 1987, ending up with the second-highest opening weekend number of the year.[5] Critical reception for the film was surprisingly positive, given the subject matter. Bullets, blood, and aliens were typically ingredients for critical demolition, and initial reviews of the movie tended to group it in with the action films of around the same time, calling it a cousin to *Rambo*, or a *Missing in Action* that morphs into *Alien* by the end. At the time, the critics weren't able to spot the sea change happening right in front of them. It's understandable, in a way, because the easy thing to do is to lump *Predator* in with all the monotonous super-solider films that had dominated the box office since early in the decade.

What else did these critics have to compare *Predator* to in 1987? Despite any similarities *Predator* may have shared with those aforementioned genre films, the more important aspect of the film was the way it subtly subverted expectations, something McTiernan would do to an even greater degree in his next movie.

6

Predator and "Taking the Piss Out" of '80s Machismo

On the surface, *Predator* looks like any other souped-up '80s action extravaganza, heavy on biceps and light on nuance. And make no mistake, it *is*. At least it's that way in the beginning. After all, this is the film where, in the opening scene, McTiernan and director of photography Donald McAlpine hold on a medium shot of Arnold Schwarzenegger's and Carl Weathers' glistening arms—seemingly carved out of sweat-soaked granite—locked in a high five that almost immediately turns into a midair arm-wrestling competition. It's the pinnacle of high-testosterone maleness, which dominated the multiplexes in Reagan's America, about as close to blatant, posturing machismo McTiernan can convey without these two actors dropping their trousers. Yes, this is still a big-time "guy" movie at its core.

But an interesting thing happens as the wheels of the *Predator* plot get spinning. The preconceived dogmas of these special forces mercenaries are subverted, not by their own actions, but by the situation in which they find themselves, brought on by the invisible killer stalking them in the jungle. Systematically, these towers of testosterone are reduced to rubble. They are skinned, heads turned to pools of blood and mass, their chests blown apart, their arms severed, and, as the Conrad-like journey deeper into the darkness beneath the jungle canopy grows more dire, all semblance of these indestructible Masters of the Universe has been upended. These '80s heroes of our capitalist imaginations are all but decimated, with only one left standing to defend what heroism remains. And even *he* is beaten to a bloody pulp.

The platoon of mercenaries is, from Schwarzenegger's Dutch on down, saturated with testosterone. This is a battalion of men brimming with confidence and an inherent bloodlust programmed in their brains by years of military service, a not-too-distant cousin of the cinematic grunts who worked alongside John Rambo, John Matrix, and Colonel James Braddock.

It doesn't take long for the story to begin to tear these men down. The discovery of a downed chopper and a friend and fellow soldier skinned, hanging upside down from the trees, takes the air out of the platoon right away. This discovery is a blow to the bristling bravado that had been carrying these soldiers, a crack in the façade of what was so carefully manicured in the opening scenes.

The mission goes according to plan in one of the film's early action set pieces, but things unravel in the aftermath, where the mission is revealed to be under false pretenses. This is yet another breakdown in the macho code of our indestructible heroes. These men have been sent into the jungle with information that has turned out to be a lie, setting them up as simple pawns on a much larger chessboard. It creates doubt, a weakness in these human mountains and military specialists, and it exposes even more of the vulnerability that began with the discovery of their fallen friend.

The second and third acts of *Predator* consist of the hunter systematically killing members of the team one by one, each death creating a different set of doubts and fears, and each signifying another move towards a new underlying ideology.

The death of Jesse Ventura's Blain is a huge blow to the virile code. Blain, sporting a Gatling gun, is the definitive macho soldier at the heart of the team, the ultimate Alpha male in a sea of Alpha males. He chides his co-workers early on for refusing a fistful of chewing tobacco, claims he "ain't got time to bleed" after he's shot, and seems impervious to the early guerrilla attackers in the initial blitz. But the predator makes quick work of Blain later on, blowing a hole in his chest the size of the knot of chew tucked in his jaw. It's easy, effortless, and it strips all the masculine posturing on which Ventura's character had been so carefully built. Even more telling is the reaction of Blain's closest friend in the unit, Mac.

Once Mac sees Blain murdered, his hardened exterior cracks wide open in what might be the most underrated performance in the film. The initial shock has Mac and his comrades opening up their machine guns, firing aimlessly and endlessly into the jungle void until their weapons are empty, the deliberate attempt by McTiernan to demystify the weapons.

to "take the piss out of war," and "quietly ridicule" action films built upon the foundation of gunfire. He is taking yet another prop of the macho code away from his Masters of the Universe.

Mac slips into an extended grieving period unheard of in movies like this. Typically, the death of a team member or a pivotal character in an action film along the lines of *Predator* is met with a few lines of anguish, then the plot moves along, not wanting to bog down in emotional reflection. This is not true for Mac, who is clearly broken by the loss of his old Vietnam buddy. Mac's sorrow is extensive and it ultimately leads to his undoing. He breaks from the unit, at least mentally, and takes it upon himself to exact revenge for Blain. It is then when Mac's self-assuredness returns, except it has a glint of madness, his mind soaked in despair and a little bit of booze. He thinks he's sharp, but he is not sharp enough, and he winds up having his head blown apart by the Predator.

These deaths have systematically dismantled this tough-guy world; the bulging biceps of Dillon and Dutch, locked in a midair arm wrestling stalemate, are but a distant memory here. Now the survivors are no longer confident, but frightened. They grow anxious as the alien hunter tightens his grip on his prey. He kills Carl Weathers' Dillon after blowing his arm off his own body, symbolically weakening the firearm as it falls to the jungle floor, rendered useless in the blink of an eye.

Billy's death is another interesting elimination of preset manhood. Billy is the token mystic of the bunch. He is a Native American who seems to live and breathe these trees and this jungle. He operates on feel more than instinct, and he is one of the first to understand what the team is up against with this alien. Near the end of the second act, Billy takes it upon himself to stay behind and battle their pursuer. He tells Dutch his plan, and Dutch practically gives him "the knowing nod."

When Billy dies, he does so off camera, his scream heard by Dutch and Anna as they try and get to the chopper. The scream is high-pitched—another clear marker in the film that these men die like any of us would in the face of such horror: helplessly shrieking in pain.

With the team decimated, it's up to Dutch to end this chaos. This is a Hollywood film, so we all know going in Schwarzenegger will come out on top. But this is not the *Commando* Schwarzenegger, nor the *Raw Deal* tough guy who is impervious to pain. This is Arnold Schwarzenegger, in this setting, barely making it out alive. He must use the environment, reorganizing his training to craft ingenious snares and traps to thwart the

Predator; but it doesn't take long for this strategy to fail him and he must square off directly with the beast.

Dutch's eventual victory comes thanks to a last-ditch outsmarting of the Predator: a log rigged to crush him if he steps in just the right place. The win is luck more than anything—that, and the Hollywood machine refusing to let Schwarzenegger lose. Yet still, the monster has to end things, killing itself in the hopes of claiming Dutch's life in the collateral damage. Even when Dutch emerges victorious, it's not due entirely to his own ingenuity.

And as we begin our narrative with a squad of big, powerful Masters of the Military Industrial Complex, with big weapons and even bigger bravado, so we end with one man and the only woman in the film, which is interesting to consider against the backdrop of 1987 when women in genre movies, save for Sigourney Weaver's Ellen Ripley in the *Alien* franchise, were almost entirely window dressing or femmes fatales.

All the testosterone that sets the stage for *Predator* is stripped away, and with it, the notion that one man, or a group of men, can overcome anything with their biceps, is subsequently destroyed. McTiernan manages to subvert expectations in one fell swoop, delivering a genuinely thrilling sci-fi adventure film for the ages, and signaling that a shift in action heroism was on its way.

7

John McTiernan, Man of Action

And then, just like that, John McTiernan almost died in the cockpit of a chartered plane.[1]

Despite the rousing success that was *Predator* in 1987—big box office, an iconic space creature, instant notoriety for everyone involved in the cast and crew—the location discrepancies ate away at McTiernan and the perfectionist he had already become with his craft. Not enough to ruin the fun he was having with a hit film and the list of offers expanding, mind you, but still enough to stick with him.

The differences between jungle settings were all he could see when he would revisit *Predator*. Trees barren, brown leaves scattered all over the ground; then, other scenes green, thick, and lush, the way a jungle is supposed to look on celluloid. The casual filmgoer wouldn't notice these sorts of background inconsistencies, and if they did they probably were not as distracted by them as McTiernan.

Regardless, McTiernan never trusted location scouts after the *Predator* issue. He decided that, moving forward, he would charter a plane he could fly and do his own location scouting. Then there would be nobody to blame if things did not turn out right.

During a scouting trip, one of the engines of his plane malfunctioned and burst into flames mid-flight. The only strategy in play was for McTiernan to send the plane into a nosedive in hopes that the vertical plummet towards the ground would put out the flames in time for him to level out and land safely. So, at fourteen thousand feet, McTiernan pointed the nose of the plane towards the earth, straight down, descending rapidly to twenty-five hundred feet before pulling the plane out of its dive and finding a nearby two-lane highway on which to land. It was the sort of thing that might happen in one of McTiernan's subsequent movies, but it had happened to him. And he handled it about as well as the heroes in his films might.

After this kind of near-death experience, most people would swear off any sort of air travel, never to get back into the cockpit again, let alone fly in any sort of airplane for the rest of their days. Not John McTiernan, who went out and bought his own plane and continued to scout his own locations into perpetuity.

PART III

Yippee Ki Yay

8
Nothing Lasts Forever

Brooklyn native Roderick Thorp attended City College of New York, where he took writing classes and worked on finding a unique voice in his prose throughout his college career. Thorp had always shown a talent for fiction, but after graduating from City College in 1957 he discovered that writing was a tough bit of business for most aspiring novelists, and not really the best way to pay the bills. His publishing progress was too slow, so he went to work at his father's business, a private detective agency.

Thorp was a burly man, bearded and imposing, a perfect fit for the private investigator business. It was in this practice where he learned about the world of investigative work, police procedures, and all manner of insider information regarding the world, the details, and the language of law enforcement. When he finally took this new knowledge and applied it to his writing, things would begin to take shape.[1]

Thorp's first novel, *Into the Forest*, was not well received, and slipped out of view almost immediately. It was his second novel, *The Detective* in 1966, which managed to find both critical and commercial success, and put Thorp on the path to a successful career as an author of hard-boiled detective novels. The story, about a private detective named Joe Leland who gets pulled into the seedy sexual underbelly of New York City, was a familiar setting for Thorp, and a simple way for him to mix the two histories of his life to that point. Thanks to the familiarity, Thorp's writing began to flow. *The Detective* was a seismic hit for the genre, and it also caught the attention of Hollywood. 20th Century–Fox acquired the rights to the book, and got to work on their adaptation.

The Detective hit theaters in 1968, and starred Frank Sinatra as Joe Leland. The film, directed by Gordon Douglas, was a hit for Fox, but nothing on par with the millions of copies of Thorp's novel still being purchased.

Still, it was enough of a hit for Fox to tell Thorp they would buy the sequel whenever he got around to writing it.

Nothing Lasts Forever features Leland, but in a much different setting than the sexually polluted underground scene in Manhattan. This time, Thorp jetted his protagonist, now in his sixties, across the country to Los Angeles to visit his career-minded daughter, Stephanie. Terrorists, led by Anton "Little Tony the Red" Gruber, take over the skyscraper in the middle of the office Christmas party, and it's up to Leland to stop them. It was a sequel the studio was ready to buy in the late 1960s, and they were ready to make it happen with Frank Sinatra back in the title role.

Then, the always-fickle Sinatra turned them down. It left the studio scrambling and Thorp's novel twisting in the wind. It wouldn't get a paperback circulation until 1979. Meanwhile, Fox held onto the rights and kept them tucked away for fifteen years until Joel Silver laid his eyes on the book.[2]

Silver decided to get this project up and running once again, and offered the role once again to Frank Sinatra, who was now seventy-three. He declined, and Silver turned to Robert Mitchum to fill Sinatra's shoes. Mitchum turned Silver down as well, claiming that all these stunts were not in the cards for a man his age. Silver was left with a hot screenplay and no lead actor. He flirted with the idea of turning *Nothing Lasts Forever* into a *Commando* sequel. It might have made sense at first given the plot of the original film, but the idea of Arnold Schwarzenegger once again having to save his daughter felt like nothing more than a thin retread of the first movie.

Perhaps spurred by Mitchum's declaration, Silver decided to make some changes to the character. This would no longer be an aging detective visiting his daughter, but a young cop visiting his wife. This alteration created avenues for bigger, more bombastic action sequences. It was a simple shift, but one that opened up a wide array of possibilities for him; and it helped begin to change the course of action cinema for the foreseeable future.

Jeb Stuart was then tasked with turning *Nothing Lasts Forever* into a workable screenplay with new, younger leads, and a compelling hook. They still needed a reason for the husband and wife to be on opposite sides of the country, and nothing was coming together for Stuart.

One day, still unable to find a solution to the *Nothing Lasts Forever* screenplay issue, Jeb Stuart and his wife got into an argument that steadily escalated. It was nothing more than a common marital squabble, a fight about something mundane that grew in size and scope for a bit until the situation was diffused. In this instance, the diffusion was Stuart storming out of the house and going for a drive to clear his head. And as he was headed down the freeway, lost in thought, a refrigerator box fell off the back of a truck right in front of his car.

Luckily for Stuart, the box was empty; the refrigerator had been delivered already. Regardless, it was a terrifying moment for him, and it put things in perspective. He thought about the fight with his wife, about how if that refrigerator box had not been empty, he may not have had a chance to make amends. It was the moment of clarity Stuart had been looking for, the perfect motivation for the characters in *Nothing Lasts Forever*. What if Leland and his wife were estranged? What if they have a fight right before the terrorists seize control? It would be another motivating factor, another reason for Leland to survive. He would be driven to make amends with his wife. It was perfect.[3]

Stuart reshaped the screenplay, and Silver brought in veteran screenwriter Steven E. de Souza to do a bit of script doctoring, small alterations and the like. The screenplay came together, but both the film's title and the lead character's name were not quite right for Silver's taste. *Nothing Lasts Forever* has a wistful quality to it; it's the title of a story about a hardened detective in the twilight of his life, not the name of an action film. And Joe Leland sounded like the world-weary gumshoe occupying the pages of Thorp's novel, not a spry young cop firing automatic weapons, igniting plastic explosives, and running barefoot across a floor littered with broken glass. They weren't even making a sequel to *The Detective* anymore, so why should they be tied to a name?

Once again, Silver turned to Shane Black, the Hollywood story fixer, for motivation. Black suggested the name of John McClane, and Silver was easily sold on the idea. But Silver also liked the name of one of the screenplays Black was working on at the time: "Die Hard." In typical Joel Silver fashion, the cogent producer convinced Black to let him use that title for *Nothing Lasts Forever*; Black agreed, and he changed the name of that "Die Hard" screenplay he was working on to "The Last Boy Scout."[4]

It was time to cast *Die Hard* and get production off the ground. Silver immediately approached John McTiernan with the project, and McTiernan saw the vehicle's potential. He agreed to direct, and they started the process of casting.

Since the age of the Joe Leland character from *Nothing Lasts Forever*, now named John McClane, had been changed to a younger cop in the film adaptation, the heavy hitters came calling.

There was Arnold Schwarzenegger, of course, who would have been the clear choice had *Die Hard* ended up a *Commando* sequel. But he did not fit here. The same went for Sylvester Stallone, Burt Reynolds, Richard Gere, Mel Gibson, all of whom showed interest in the project before ultimately passing on it. Harrison Ford lobbied briefly for the role, but the talks never went beyond that. Besides, McTiernan and Silver wanted to go a different direction with the character. They wanted McClane to be more of a normal guy, less chiseled physically, and they wanted an actor who would convincingly carry a bit of emotional baggage across the country with him. Silver convinced the studio to let them hire a little-known television comedy actor named Bruce Willis.

As a teen, Bruce Willis found the theater stage at Penn's Grove High School in the blue-collar suburb of Carneys Point Township, New Jersey, the only place where he could break free of a stutter. But he didn't pursue acting right after graduation, trying his hand both as a security guard at a nuclear power plant, and, later, as a private detective. These jobs did not stick with Willis, so he enrolled in a drama program at Montclair State University. Willis had an unconventional handsomeness, a rugged New Jersey charm, and his blue-collar attitude, his sardonic sense of humor, and his wry smile would begin to stand out at Montclair.

He found some success working in off-Broadway plays for a few years after graduating, and he grabbed walk-on roles on *Miami Vice* and *The Twilight Zone*. One day he auditioned for the role of a character named David Addison in a forthcoming TV series titled *Moonlighting*. He would play the romantic counterpart and professional peer of Maddie Hayes, played by Cybil Shepherd. Willis beat out hundreds of hopefuls for the role, and the ABC series became a hit for the network and its stars. It established Bruce Willis as a comedic talent.

Legendary director Blake Edwards cast Willis in two separate films in 1987. The first, *Blind Date*, featured Willis courting an unhinged Kim Basinger. It was no critical darling, and Willis's put-upon yuppie felt like merely an extension of his David Addison character; nevertheless, *Blind Date* was a popular film.[5] *Sunset*, the second Edwards/Willis collaboration, did not fare as well. The story has legendary Western actor Tom Mix (Willis) teaming up with an aging Wyatt Earp (James Garner) to solve a murder.

Critics and audiences rejected the tonally inconsistent comedy/drama, and *Sunset* failed at the box office upon its release in 1988.

Attrition was the only way Willis landed the McClane role. McTiernan and Steven E. de Souza were reaching when they called him to come read for the part. With no proven track record of success in film, and no background in action movies or stunt work, Willis seemed on the surface like a complete mismatch. But he fit McTiernan's plan, and he sold the part in his audition.

With Bruce Willis in place as the hero, McTiernan needed to find his villain, now named Hans Gruber in the screenplay instead of "Little Tony the Red." Rather than recycling famous villains of action films past, or seeking out a big name to help boost potential box-office numbers, McTiernan and Joel Silver had an unknown in mind. They had seen this gifted individual onstage in London, playing the villainous Valmont in *Dangerous Liaisons*, a perfect match for the sort of well-mannered scoundrel McTiernan wanted in his movie. His name was Alan Rickman.[6]

Born February 21, 1946, in West London, Alan Rickman, the second of four children, turned to art as a way of escaping his tough upbringing. Alan's father was a factory worker, and his mother a housewife. His father died when Alan was only eight years old, and the family struggled to make ends meet.

After appearing in plays during his school years, Alan Rickman turned his attention to set decoration and graphic design for a while to ensure a steadier income than acting would offer. In 1978, he joined the Royal Shakespeare Company, and built a solid stage career before turning to BBC serials and other opportunities in London's theater world. It was then that he landed the role of Valmont in *Dangerous Liaisons*, and Hollywood came calling.[7]

Rickman famously said, on multiple occasions, that he was in Los Angeles only two days when McTiernan and Silver offered him the role of Hans Gruber. He was a stage actor across the pond with no film experience, and he almost declined the role outright. His first reaction after reading the script: "What the hell is this? I'm not doing an action movie."[8]

But Rickman began to think about the screenplay, to dig into the story a bit deeper, and he found the wit and progressive nature of some of the characters to be refreshing. He found it especially interesting that the African American characters in the story were more than simply inserted into the story for the sake of diversity. Rickman appreciated this approach, one that was, sadly, a rarity in the late 1980s.

It was enough to convince Rickman to accept the role, but despite being a Hollywood greenhorn, he would try to give his own input on what he thought the Gruber character should be and what he should do. He had two big ideas: have Gruber wear suits rather than some version of the fatigues and casual clothing the other terrorists wear, and at some point in the film pretend to be a hostage.

He ran the changes past Joel Silver, the notorious tyrant, who told him in so many words to shut his mouth, and that he will wear what he's told. Even though that meeting may not have gone according to plan, when Rickman returned to the set the next day he found the scene where he pretends to be an escaped hostage there in the second act.

Silver and McTiernan realized the risks they were taking by hiring a fledgling comedy TV actor and stage actor from Europe to lead their big-budget, tent-pole action film. With modern eyes, and the advantage of hindsight, Willis and Rickman look like a dream team of hero and villain. Before *Die Hard* hit theaters, however, their names held almost no weight in Hollywood. Nevertheless, McTiernan knew he had the right men for the job.

McTiernan, Silver, Larry Gordon, and casting director Jackie Burch also needed to find the perfect actress to play Holly Gennaro, the strong-willed career woman who has no problem pushing back against John McClane's antiquated idea of marriage and his desire for her to come back to New York despite her work. Holly would need to be confident, almost masculine, given her surroundings. Willis suggested Bonnie Bedelia, a native of New York who had been acting since the age of three.

Bedelia had built a sturdy career acting in television movies throughout the 1970s, but it was her work as a drag racer in the 1983 film *Heart Like a Wheel* that caught Willis's attention. In her performance, Willis saw the sort of powerful female lead who would fit perfectly alongside the blue-collar John McClane. On Willis's suggestion, Silver and McTiernan brought her in to audition. It was evident almost immediately that Bedelia was everything they wanted and needed in their Holly Gennaro. Bedelia could shift from emotional and soft to cold and biting in a heartbeat, and this range would prove most beneficial in the pivotal argument scene between Holly and John.

As for the terrorists, McTiernan wanted the majority of them to be a mixture of both faceless, interchangeable goons and glamorous European henchmen. The only discernable terrorist in the bunch would be Karl, the second in command who is driven to the edge of madness by McClane, who kills his brother early in the film. McTiernan went with Alexander Godunov, a Russian ballet dancer who had appeared in only a handful of supporting roles; but his large frame and golden locks personified the European allure McTiernan wanted to see in a few of the supporting villains.

The fourth lead of the film was Sergeant Al Powell, a Los Angeles beat cop who stumbles into the terrorist takeover and becomes McClane's closest ally over the radio waves. McTiernan and Burch agreed on character actor Reginald VelJohnson, who had a handful of bit parts and minor roles to his credit.

Several peripheral players were added to inject humor into the story so as not to weigh down the film with relentless action. For example, Paul Gleason, the oafish principal from *The Breakfast Club*, was hired as the annoyingly skeptical police chief outside Nakatomi Tower, primarily because of his ability to make any scenario absurd.

And then there was Hart Bochner, hired to play the tactless, stereotypical, cocaine-snorting executive Harry Ellis, who gets in over his head in a one-on-one meeting with Gruber in the film's second act. Bochner had spent his career playing the straight versions of these drug-addled executives and stiffs in television and theatrical features, so he jumped at the chance to send up these characters with a broad, borderline satirical take on the 1980s businessman.

McTiernan assembled a cast full of memorable faces to perform even the most mundane tasks. Everyone who pushes the plot forward, save for the generic background thugs in Gruber's band of thieves, carried a uniqueness in their faces, so there would be no question as to who was doing what, and for what reason.

With the cast and crew ready to go, McTiernan began principal photography on *Die Hard* on November 2, 1987.

9

An Ode to Joy, Not Terror

John McTiernan knew he had to change the motives of the terrorists in *Nothing Lasts Forever*. He detailed in the film's commentary track that he wanted *Die Hard* to be a fun, summer action-adventure film, and he realized using terrorists motivated by politics would be anything but fun. Traditional terrorists in the geopolitical realm, driven to kill and conquer because of their dogma, are all too real and threatening and somber; injecting any humor, or "joy," as McTiernan continuously referenced, into a dark tale of terrorists would be too tough to sell to summer audiences seeking escapism.

But thieves, on the other hand, thieves would play. Because who doesn't love a clever heist film on a grand scale?[1]

Changing the plot from a straight terrorist takeover to a heist was a large brush stroke that changed the tone of the story; from there, McTiernan made sure to add little details during the shoot to keep the mood as light as possible and keep the Christmas season theme visible in the margins. This lighthearted injection filling in the extraneous details of the film would help to not exhaust the audience with relentless, serious action from start to finish.

McTiernan had characters hum notes to Christmas songs, he had composer Michael Kaman thread his prickly score with little Yuletide hints, and he made sure to add small moments of humor—like Al Leong's henchman swiping a candy bar in the lobby before kneecapping an entire SWAT team—to bring out some smiles amid all the chaos. After all, this was supposed to be entertaining above all else.

While McTiernan used a bit of his European influence in *Predator*, implementing moving cuts and allowing the camera to play a part in the story whenever possible, he felt *Die Hard* would need even more motion (despite the fact that editors would push back from time to time during post-production). A story inside a confined space like a skyscraper would flow better if the camera were as fluid as possible. Donald McAlpine had served as McTiernan's director of photography on *Predator*, but McTiernan wanted someone with whom he could incorporate the moving cuts more frequently. He needed someone influenced by European cinema much like he had been, so he hired a Dutch cinematographer named Jan de Bont.

Jan de Bont had been working as a cameraman since the mid–1960s, mostly in European films where he first gained notoriety on *Turkish Delight*, a drama directed by Dutch filmmaker Paul Verhoeven. The two would work on several films over the next few years, and it was de Bont's work on Verhoeven's *The 4th Man*, an erotic thriller from 1983, that most caught McTiernan's eye and led him to the hire.

McTiernan and de Bont butted heads throughout the shoot. The two strong personalities, one a tough New Yorker, the other a hot-headed Dutchman, would bicker through compositions at times, enough to concern the crew as they watched these two Alpha males fighting for what they felt was the correct shot. But the squabbling would soon end and the director and cameraman would find common ground for the betterment of the picture. No matter what they would argue about during the shoot, McTiernan and de Bont knew *Die Hard* would benefit from the creative European techniques that had been nonexistent in American action cinema. In this, they could find common ground.

Speaking of that European influence, McTiernan leaned into Ján Kadár's tutelage regarding film as a piece of music. It should contain movements, capture moods, transition in the manner of classical concertos and operas. Swish pans in different settings, all lined up back to back, would work like movements in music, capturing transition and mood simultaneously, giving every inch of the film undeniable kinetics. McTiernan and de Bont were in lock-step on this approach, but the editors found the task a bit more problematic.

It may sound easy enough, splicing a film together. But the moving cut was a technique unfamiliar to many American editors. Gradually, McTiernan and his editors, John F. Link and Frank J. Urioste, would find a rhythm in the *Die Hard* editing room, and the cuts would begin to speak to them as they put the finished product together. But it took time.

What's more, the movie was set to have a number of scenes where

John McTiernan (center) discusses a scene with Grand L. Bush (left) and Robert Davi on the set of *Die Hard* (20th Century–Fox, 1988).

conversations and dialogue occurred over telephones and radios between police officers, terrorists, and McClane. To help give these scenes a sense of true conversational flow, of spatial geography that would work for the audience and keep them engaged, McTiernan detailed in the commentary how he would frame one character on the left of the screen and the other on the right to visually imply they were speaking to one another, despite the fact that they were in different locations.

For example, the scene where Hart Bochner's Harry Ellis tries to smooth talk his way into the good graces of Hans by turning over John McClane—only to be exposed as a fraud and subsequently murdered—McTiernan uses some clever blocking to make the three-way conversation flow visually. When Gruber is speaking to McClane, the two men are facing each other in their respective settings; when Gruber hands Ellis the radio, Ellis is on the right of the frame looking left. It is here that McClane shifts in his own setting, moving to the left of the frame where he can face right. This way, as the scene intercuts, it has the feeling of the two men talking to each other in the same space.

9. An Ode to Joy, Not Terror

These are the sorts of details McTiernan fought to include in *Die Hard* to give it a recognizable personality, because he wanted more than anything to weave his unique tutelage into an action film of this magnitude.

Another element McTiernan incorporated into the story involved the way he took in foreign films as a youth. He never watched the subtitles, but instead read the faces and listened to the inflections in characters' line deliveries. In *Die Hard*, the terrorists speak gibberish, no real language, but something that sounded vaguely enough like Eastern European vocabulary. What the terrorists were saying was not crucial; it was *how* they were saying it that mattered.

Something that sold McTiernan on the film from the start, and a small detail he wanted to keep in the film, was an early character-building moment for John McClane: riding in the front of the limo with Argyle (De'voreaux White), whose character McTiernan compares to the chorus in *Henry V*. It showed that McClane was not fit for this sort of luxurious welcome from the Nakatomi Corporation. He was not about to sit miles away from Argyle in the backseat being chauffeured around town like someone he's not.

This little detail, McTiernan knew, would go a long way in defining McClane in these early scenes. It would also emphasize the fish-out-of-water stigma that is perhaps the character's most endearing trait, outside of his sardonic humor and quick thinking. Willis's blue-collar background sells the moment.

McTiernan also tried his best to shoot the movie in some sort of linear order, at least managing to cover the early setup scenes, the calm before the storm, before getting into any of the action. If they had to bounce back and forth between these tempered, more domestic scenes of John and Holly, and elevator shafts exploding and shattered glass underfoot, McTiernan was certain the rhythm and chemistry would be off between Willis and Bedelia, and the characters would have a tougher time finding the appropriate rhythm.

Twentieth Century–Fox was happy to use its own building in Los Angeles as Nakatomi Plaza. It sounded like a terrific plan on paper, and a money-saving maneuver to top it off. Little did they know, however, the plans McTiernan and Joel Silver had in mind for the building, a geometric, postmodern skyscraper created by architects William Pereira, Bill Fain, and Scott Johnson. Several of the explosions were actually executed on site, like the rooftop fireball McClane escapes via fire hose. Some larger ones—the C-4 down the elevator shaft, for example—were shot using a barrage of flash bulbs. Fire and sound was added in post-production.

One of the toughest negotiations McTiernan and Silver had to go through would wind up being one of the most minor shots to take place outside the Fox building. It involved the LAPD tactical tank vehicle charging up the steps of the skyscraper before getting blasted by a rocket launcher. The vehicle destroying the railing running along the staircase took hours of tense negotiation. Eventually, they got it done, though they had to pay a substantial repair bill.

For all its moving parts, its massive cast, and the major set pieces needing months of prep time, the *Die Hard* shoot went off with relative smoothness. While McTiernan and Joel Silver ultimately wore each other down, their different approaches to the story worked. Production designer Jackson De Govia claimed that Silver's penchant for grand scale and scope—realism and plausibility be damned—coupled with McTiernan's desire for the action to remain as believable and grounded as humanly possible, was the perfect marriage on this particular set.

The marriage would not last beyond *Die Hard* (as was the case with Silver and directors more often than not), but the pairing was serendipitous in 1987.

10
Nakatomi Nuance

Die Hard is not only the best tangential Christmas film out there, it is the closest thing cinema has seen to *the* perfect action movie. From top to bottom, the confluence of thrilling set pieces, raw performances from Bruce Willis and Alan Rickman, and a fat-free screenplay, *Die Hard* will forever be the litmus test for any other action spectacles.

What sets *Die Hard* apart from the mass of action movies in its wake is the film's nuance, the little extra touches of humor and humanity filling out the story and breathing life into the characters. More than anything, *Die Hard* has more layers than just about any movie in the genre, full of real human consequences and proper motivations for the action and violence. It's these small details that work to build up to a whole, complete picture.

Think about the setup. John McClane, the dogged New York cop pays a visit to his estranged wife, Holly, in sunny Los Angeles for Christmas. His intent is to see the kids and to hopefully mend fences with Holly and find some sort of common ground, though his ego and the old-world chauvinism ingrained into his working-class psyche won't allow such compromise. And John and Holly have issues running deeper than any Christmas visit could possibly repair. The conflict in their relationship stems from Holly's dogged determination to be a career woman, and this freedom is a threat to McClane's old-school machismo. Her progressive character is a wonderful departure from the damsel-in-distress archetype. Holly's independence emasculates John almost immediately.

This creates a pathway for the audience to follow, and ultimately identify with, McClane. He is our hero, we recognize as an audience, but he has a weakness. He is a human and he is dealing with some heavy emotional strife before we even hear the first bullet fired. It builds tension beyond simple action-storytelling beats, and it pushes audiences to not only root for John McClane but also empathize with him and his shaky domestic situation. John wants to rescue his wife when Gruber's team invades; he wants to make amends, and in the moments of despair that consume John throughout the film, he carries on with this deep-seated desire to get one last chance to tell Holly he's sorry and that he loves her.

The audience wants McClane to kill Hans Gruber and save the day, but they are also hoping he gets his opportunity to tell Holly he's sorry.

McTiernan uses the camera as much as the characters to tell the story, pulling the viewer into the cramped ductwork and never-ending elevator shaft of Nakatomi Plaza. The camera moves and ducks and slides, and tension builds through cramped quarters and desperation. McTiernan and Jan de Bont capture it all like a concerto, which was one of McTiernan's motivations from the start.

As big as the action set pieces are in *Die Hard*, the small personal moments and tense conversations between McClane and Gruber—many of which are heard via radio—are equally as impactful. Part of the credit belongs to Willis and Rickman, who play beautifully off each other. Our hero, a working-class New Jersey cop, faces off against a sleek European thief with a carefully manicured beard and designer suits. The dichotomy is serendipitous.

Rickman's presence in *Die Hard* gives the movie an art-house sensibility amidst all the carnage and chaos, most notably in the quiet scene he and McClane share in the empty floor near the Nakatomi rooftop, where McClane catches him snooping for detonators. Gruber pretends to be an escaped hostage—the aforementioned idea he had run by Silver in the early days of production.

Without McTiernan's awareness of the importance in this moment, his deft ability to slow everything down and create the perfect brief beat of intimacy between these two as they finally meet face to face, this conversation may have been overlooked in order to simply move the action forward; lesser action films would have sent this scene to the cutting-room floor early in the process. It is one of the many quiet moments, oddly enough, that define *Die Hard* as something transcendent of its own genre.

Die Hard was a new breed of action film with a new hero. But, as Alfred Hitchcock once said in so many words, a film is only as good as its villain. In *Die Hard*, McTiernan introduced the world to a new standard in snarling villainy.

10. Nakatomi Nuance

Cinematographer Jan de Bont (left), John McTiernan and Bruce Willis work through the climactic scene in *Die Hard* (20th Century–Fox, 1988).

Think where *First Blood* would be without Brian Dennehy's unforgiving small-town Sheriff Teasle, or *Commando* without the crazed Freddie Mercury doppelgänger, Bennett (Vernon Wells). In *Die Hard*, Hans Gruber has time to percolate with the audience; he has flair, he is impeccable in his John Phillips suit, a villain from a James Bond picture grounded in this very real setting. He may even be a little too charming when he is killing Takagi or threatening screaming hostages. That speaks to the nuance of Rickman's performance. He manages to slowly and steadily devolve from even-tempered and arrogant to manic and theatrical, and captures every new emotional setting for the character at the right times. It is the most crucial role in the original film, and a role with which the franchise has struggled mightily in the sequels. William Sadler was a militaristic robot, cold and distant in *Die Hard 2*. *Live Free or Die Hard* had a practically nonexistent Timothy Olyphant as its central villain; with *A Good Day to Die Hard*, the identity of the true villain is anybody's guess.

The nuances, the performances, and the quieter moments are all terrific in their ability to help construct a world in which the audience is fully invested; but make no mistake, *Die Hard* is still an action film, first and foremost, containing some of the most exciting sequences in the genre.

The penultimate sequence, of McClane leaping from the edge of an exploding rooftop, is arguably the film's most memorable; it is a sequence masterfully crafted with McClane's incredible desperation and McTiernan's adherence to never letting his protagonist escape easily from any predicament. We consider the possible consequence he faces, pinned down in a corner on the rooftop, with mere seconds to make a decision. We feel the weight and pull of the fire hose as he ties it around his waist, and that iconic shot of McClane flying through the air, a fireball exploding behind his silhouette, is exhilarating.

The best films of any genre fit together like pieces of a puzzle; such is the case with *Die Hard*. McTiernan, the action beats in mind, masterfully injects the nuance to bridge such moments together. He earns the trust of the audience early on, after which he can take the story in any number of directions.

The audience will come along for the ride.

11
The New Action Template

The mark of a truly influential piece of filmmaking is the imitation in its wake. The success of George Lucas's *Star Wars* created a cottage industry for young filmmakers who wanted to try their hand at their very own space opera. In horror, *Halloween*'s Michael Myers birthed slashers Jason and Freddy in the early 1980s.

Think about the way Quentin Tarantino's *Pulp Fiction* turned Hollywood upside-down in 1994, the way every film student and wannabe at the time had their own non-linear, dialogue-laden crime saga full of rich and morally bankrupt characters they wanted to show us in the hopes it would have the same effect on their careers. The *Pulp Fiction* imitators, from *Things to Do in Denver When You're Dead*, to *2 Days in the Valley*, to *The Way of the Gun*, were most certainly the highest form of flattery for Tarantino's work, even if none of these lookalikes ever came close to the power of the film they were imitating.

A few years before *Pulp Fiction* changed the crime-drama, *Die Hard* did the same thing to the action genre.

A week or two before its official theatrical release on July 15, 1988, McTiernan, Silver, Gordon, and 20th Century–Fox executive Tom Sherak hosted a small screening in Mountain View, California. They gathered together roughly five hundred citizens of the small Northern California town, asking them if they wanted to go check out an action movie with Bruce Willis from *Moonlighting*. When the screening ended, the audience erupted in applause and one younger gentleman from the back of the theater stood up and shouted, "Play it again!" McTiernan and his producers knew they had something special on their hands.[1]

Die Hard was an unmitigated success. Critics generally praised it, which was a surprise in and of itself for a big, loud, summer action-explosion fest. There were a few dissenters, including Roger Ebert's bafflingly misguided pan of the film, based almost solely on the performance of Paul Gleason as the bumbling police chief Robinson.[2] But even Ebert's critical words did not have the strength to hurt this film.

Die Hard opened third at the box office on July 22, 1988, on the heels of a limited release the week before, with just over $7 million. It may not sound impressive, but it was up against the family-friendly smash hit *Who Framed Roger Rabbit?*—the Robert Zemeckis marriage of cartoon and live-action characters was enjoying its fifth consecutive week at number one—and Eddie Murphy at the height of his powers in *Coming to America*. The number was not disappointing, especially for an action movie with a TV star and an unknown stage actor from Europe headlining the film. Besides, this very adult thriller, in the middle of the summer, would prove to have some legs. The opening weekend number was not nearly as impressive as *Die Hard*'s staying power.

The next week, McTiernan's movie checked in at number four; then,

John McClane leaps from the exploding rooftop in the most harrowing action scene in *Die Hard* (20th Century–Fox, 1988).

it was number three for several weeks. It peaked at number two in September, almost two months after its initial release (these were decidedly different times at the box office) and ended its sixteen-week run with just over $83 million, on a $28 million budget. Adjusted for inflation, that's right at $175 million.[3]

For years and years, and even to this day, *Die Hard* imitators come and go. There were some admirable entries in this subgenre along the way—most surprisingly, the Jean-Claude Van Damme "*Die Hard*-at-a-hockey-game" thriller, *Sudden Death*, and Steven Seagal's *Under Siege*, which took the action to a battleship. Others, like the boarding school hostage-actioner *Toy Soldiers* starring Sean Astin and Louis Gossett, Jr., fared much worse and were swiftly pushed out of view, rarely to be heard from again.

Bruce Willis was officially a star, one of the most sought-after fresh faces in the industry. Alan Rickman was a star as well, and for years would be the go-to villain for a wide variety of genre films. And John McTiernan had made it as a filmmaker, securing his spot as the new voice of action cinema. He had his second boot on the ground now, and Hollywood opened up in front of his eyes.

But nothing lasts forever.

Part IV

The Connery Years

12

The Clancy Phenomenon

Nineteen eighty-eight was a big year for John McTiernan. Outside of his life-changing success that was *Die Hard*, in November he married Donna Dubrow, his second wife and a producer who would also work alongside him on 1992's *Medicine Man*.

Following the watershed triumph of *Die Hard*, a sequel was inevitable. And McTiernan was on board, or at least he was willing to direct in the beginning. But this was the late 1980s, and big studio sequels didn't move at the blinding pace they do today.

Once upon a time in Hollywood, sequels were given half the budget of their predecessor, not double. Old-school franchises like the Universal monster movies trimmed their overhead, as *Dracula* became *House of Dracula*, *Frankenstein* turned into *House of Frankenstein*, and the quality dissipated right along with the budget. The late 1960s and early 1970s saw budgets for the *Planet of the Apes* franchise dwindle to a point where the makeup effects became laughable, many extras simply wearing obvious rubber masks instead of more expensive prosthetics; and the stories in the *Apes* sequels fared just as poorly.

It was not until the critical and commercial success of Francis Ford Coppola's *The Godfather Part II*, the first sequel to earn an Academy Award nomination (and subsequent win) for Best Picture, coupled with the mid–'70s birth of summer blockbusters, that the sequel game was seen as a big-business opportunity. Even then, movies were not necessarily released with their sequel already in pre-production the way they are in modern Hollywood. Success was still important.

In the waning years of the 1980s, studios had seen their new franchising business model succeed with the likes of *Jaws*, *Star Wars*, and the *Indiana Jones* films, among others. All of those pictures were subsequently given sequels, but only after the original was a hit. The latter years of the decade was a time in place nestled in between the cash grab, on-the-cheap sequel methodology of the past and the modern way of studio filmmaking in the twenty-first century.

With McTiernan still a relatively unproven commodity and Bruce Willis a rookie going into *Die Hard*, the studio and Joel Silver played the long game. They waited for the numbers, the buzz, the praise, and Willis's star to shoot through the ceiling of preconceived action heroes before moving forward with *Die Hard 2: Die Harder*. But in that downtime, McTiernan spotted another project he had been wanting to work on for a few years—and one that would keep him away from producer Joel Silver, whom McTiernan had found increasingly difficult to work with after the back-to-back productions of *Predator* and *Die Hard*.

Personality clashes aside, McTiernan saw an opportunity to pivot with this new project. It was a chance to test his evolution as a director, to flex all new muscles and hopefully continue to weave the European influences of his education into the tapestry of his blockbusters.

This new project would be another action film, at least on the surface; it was much more focused on military strategy, intellect, and quiet moments of tension in place of gunfire, bloodshed, and one-liners. McTiernan took on the project, leaving *Die Hard 2* in the hands of a fresh-faced action filmmaker from Finland named Renny Harlin.[1]

The Hunt for Red October was the first novel from Baltimore author Tom Clancy. In his youth, Clancy wanted to be a part of the military, getting as far as joining the army reserves during his college years at Loyola University. But he had severe nearsightedness, so much so that he could never continue his military aspirations beyond the reserves. Instead, much like Roderick Thorp, Clancy took his English background and extensive military knowledge and passion and turned it into one of the most successful writing careers in American history.

By the time *The Hunt for Red October* was to be adapted for the screen, Tom Clancy had collided headfirst with the zeitgeist of American popular culture, having produced four espionage thrillers, all bestsellers. His books were everywhere across the globe, in airplanes and on beaches and wherever eager fans could squeeze in a chapter; the enthusiasm surrounding his work placed even bigger expectations on a film adaptation of his first novel.

Red October had caught McTiernan's attention when he first read the book, around the time he'd begun shooting *Predator*; but producer Mace Neufeld had already optioned the rights. Luckily for McTiernan, Neufeld and his producing partners saw the work the director was putting in on *Predator* and kept him in mind once they got their *Red October* adaptation off the ground.[2]

The book, published in 1984, took place in the middle of the Cold War and involved a rogue Russian submarine captain who had stolen a state-of-the-art Russian sub and was headed for the American coast. Was his intention to attack the United States? That's the general consensus among the military brass. But a CIA analyst and former marine named Jack Ryan believes this legend in the submarine community might be actually defecting to the United States.

The Hunt for Red October is a story built almost exclusively on the fundamentals of tension and suspense, and the action takes a backseat to extensive exposition and military jargon. The dramatic propulsion comes in the words spoken, the motives of certain characters, and the snap decisions of at least a dozen people as the narrative unfolds. It was also an incredibly intimidating work of fiction for screenwriter Larry Ferguson to adapt into a screenplay.

Ferguson, who was coming off the successes of *Beverly Hills Cop II* in 1987 and a small military thriller titled *The Presidio* in 1988, was tasked with adapting the novel into a working script. Clancy, notoriously detailed in his writing, would spill hundreds of words over the most minute details in his novels. These small details were what made the books work so well, but Ferguson knew he would have to trim away much of these expository passages to try and avoid a seven-hour movie. His first draft was built more in the spirit of Clancy's novel than a direct, faithful adaptation.

McTiernan read Ferguson's screenplay, and told him that he loved what he had done; he also told him he did not want to use a single page.

The story Ferguson was telling in his script was not what McTiernan had in mind. He wanted this story to be as close to the source material as humanly possible, as technically in depth as Paramount executives would allow in a big studio action thriller, and he saw something lying under Clancy's words that he wanted to incorporate into his version of the story: this was, to McTiernan, *Treasure Island*.

Robert Louis Stevenson's 1883 novel is a high-seas adventure, a story about mutiny and tension aboard a vessel making its way to a secret stash of buried gold. There are certainly elements in Stevenson's story that make sense within the context of Clancy's pages, and McTiernan saw this comparison as an opportunity to heighten the adventure elements. Thankfully, Larry Ferguson was not the sort of writer who let his ego get in the way of a better idea, so he and McTiernan sat down together and found their way through the story until they wound up with a proper shooting script.

With the screenplay out of the way and McTiernan on board to direct, Mace Neufeld now set about trying to find the right person to play Jack Ryan. He immediately thought of Kevin Costner, one of the hottest stars of the time and fresh off a trifecta of sizeable hits: Brian De Palma's gangster epic *The Untouchables*, and a pair of wildly popular baseball movies: *Bull Durham* and *Field of Dreams*.

Costner had the directness to play a CIA agent; he had the handsomeness to lead the film, and just a couple of years earlier he had played a double-crossing naval officer in Roger Donaldson's thriller *No Way Out*. Neufeld reached out to him, but Costner was neck-deep in a Western about which he was passionate. He simply did not have the time, so Neufeld moved on.[3]

Still wanting to find a fresh up-and-coming star to take over as Jack Ryan, in what was already being planned as a franchise for Paramount Pictures (especially since Tom Clancy had already published the second Jack Ryan novel, *Patriot Games*, in 1987), Neufeld turned his attention to an intense young actor named Alec Baldwin.

In 1990, Alec Baldwin had already acted in dozens of television shows and films, but rarely had he been the star. The closest he had come was in Tim Burton's quirky afterlife fantasy/comedy/horror mashup *Beetlejuice*, but even there the title role belonged to Michael Keaton. Otherwise, Baldwin had been the best friend, or the brother, or a member of an ensemble. But Neufeld played off a hunch he had that this polished, raven-haired young actor with the thousand-mile stare had star potential. He brought Baldwin in to meet with McTiernan and read for the part. McTiernan loved his intensity and hired him on the spot.

With Alec Baldwin, McTiernan had another opportunity to redefine the modern action star. Baldwin, like Willis, did not fit into the prototypical action-hero design, which may explain why he had not had his breakthrough performance yet. Jack Ryan is a man of action, but he is an intellectual first and foremost; this hero would explore each and every angle before resorting to physicality.

12. The Clancy Phenomenon

McTiernan saw the perfect balance of dashing good looks and intelligence in Baldwin. And Baldwin, who had an uncanny ability to memorize pages upon pages of his dialogue prior to shooting (therein making McTiernan's job that much easier), would be able to convey the emotions of Ryan—often times scared, but in the company of men who know no such emotion—with a simple facial contortion, a pursing of the lips, or trying desperately to hide the panic in his eyes. Baldwin was also game for any of the physical action his character needed to do, including an early scene outside the surfaced U.S.S. *Dallas*, which Ryan has to board from a chopper. It was Baldwin's idea to perform the stunt himself, and McTiernan was more than willing to let him. Having the actor perform the stunts was always preferred, because the scene would appear more authentic.

Jack Ryan was not the only lead in *The Hunt for Red October*; some may say he is not even the lead at all. Instead, that designation belonged to Marko Ramius, the Russian submarine captain with whom Ryan would face off. Neufeld initially hired an Austrian actor named Klaus Maria Brandauer to play Ramius. Even though Brandauer was committed to a period epic about the French Revolution, he agreed to star in *Red October* with the belief (or the hope) he could balance both films. Two weeks into the shoot, however, Brandauer realized he could not balance both films given the logistical nightmares they were causing. He was forced to back out of the Ramius part as he had agreed to the French war film first, leaving Neufeld and McTiernan behind the eight ball.

Desperate for a replacement, McTiernan took a chance and faxed a copy of the script to Sean Connery. Fresh off his first and only Academy Award win in 1988, a Supporting Actor Oscar for his role as Malone in *The Untouchables*, and hot on the heels of his turn as Harrison Ford's father in *Indiana Jones and the last Crusade*, Connery was a major player in the Hollywood system. If he agreed to take over the Ramius role it would greatly change the complexion of the film.

Connery had some reservations, mostly due to the fact that it was a Cold War thriller, and the Cold War had just ended. It turned out that the first page of the script, which would have told Connery the film takes place *before* the end of the Cold War, did not go through in the fax transmission. Once he was apprised of the update, Connery agreed to take over for Brandauer. He arrived in Los Angeles on a Friday, and his part in the film was set to begin the following Monday. With only a day or so's worth of rehearsal and preparation for the role, Connery seamlessly stepped aboard the *Red October* as General Ramius.[4]

McTiernan filled out the supporting roles much like he did in *Predator* and *Die Hard*, with unique faces and strong performers to help keep the moving parts and frequent scene changes as clear as possible. Ramius's comrades on the *Red October* included venerable characters actors Sam Neill and Tim Curry; Scott Glenn and Courtney B. Vance led the members of the American submarine, the U.S.S. *Dallas*.

On April 3, 1989, McTiernan and his cast and crew headed out to sea.

The sets of *The Hunt for Red October* proved to be the biggest hurdles for McTiernan and his crew. Aside from early scenes inside Jack Ryan's home and meeting rooms inside CIA headquarters, the bulk of the story takes place inside two submarines. These two narrow, claustrophobic metal submarine sets were problematic early on, because they were tough to negotiate for complicated scenes, and they both looked like metal tubes. There was very little early on to differentiate between the two, so McTiernan had to figure out some way to visually tell the audience which submarine they were in at a given time.

He and cinematographer Jan de Bont who, despite the contentious times he and McTiernan endured during the *Die Hard* shoot, had teamed up with the director once again, decided unique lighting schemes for each submarine would be the easiest, most surefire way to individualize the sets and make them distinguishable for audiences. The sets of the *Red October* would be, of course, backlit in a harsher red palette, and the U.S.S. *Dallas* lit in softer blues and whites.

McTiernan also needed to figure out the best way to shoot the exterior underwater sub scenes, as the cat-and-mouse between the two vessels would intensify throughout the film and each one would have to fight through navigation issues in the depths of the ocean. He decided not to film the submarines in water at all, but on a sound stage with thick clouds of smoke around the models that would give off the illusion of deep-sea opacity.

Action set pieces and special effects were secondary in the film, which was a new approach for McTiernan. It was a different way to tell a story in a familiar genre, but it still played to one of his strengths: building tension and allowing the action to grow organically. Even in the success of both *Predator* and *Die Hard*, McTiernan used his precise timing and camera work to build the optimal amount of unease before unleashing explosions and gunfire. This time around, pressure would be the modus operandi from start to finish. There were moments for action, all of which were heavy with the weight of consequence. The bulk of the excitement in the depths of the ocean were often conveyed by the sideways glances between adversaries trying their best to outsmart one another.

McTiernan made sure to subtly emphasize Ryan's intelligence early in the film, filling his home with all manner of academia, walls of leather-bound books, a domestic setup packed to the gills with worldly intelligence and educational prestige. Jack Ryan, much like John McClane, is a normal hero, but a normal hero in a drastically different setting. This "normal" hero is a milquetoast in a world with which most of us are unfamiliar: high-level government operations and darkened CIA conference rooms. He is the bookworm who has to use his intelligence to try and talk down a room full of decorated generals dead set on acting on emotion, using their gut feelings and naturally combative problem-solving skills. They are eager to engage Ramius as his submarine inches closer to the shores off Washington, D.C., and Ryan must quell their instincts.

Hiring Connery as Ramius turned out to fit the sort of story McTiernan wanted to tell. Connery, like all the major players aboard the *Red October*, was not Russian or even Austrian. Sam Neill and Tim Curry were, respectively, New Zealand and British actors. But it didn't matter because McTiernan's intention was never to tell a story with linguistic or ethnic accuracy.

In the early scenes as the submarine is descending into the depths of the ocean, Ramius and his comrades are speaking to each other in Russian; but a conversation between Ramius and Ivan Putin (Joss Ackland), the appointed political officer on board charged with relaying updates of their mission back to the Kremlin, switches mid-stream into English. It is a purposeful change, one McTiernan emphasizes by pushing in on Ackland's mouth as he reads a soliloquy. Near the middle of this monologue, Ackland speaks the word "Armageddon," which is pronounced the same in both English and Russian. Here, the Russian dialogue transitions to English and McTiernan pulls the camera back to the static, medium shot of these two men having a conversation. It is a clever, subtle way of shifting attention from the captions running along the bottom of the screen to the actors and their performances.

Ackland's monologue ends with "It is done," a clever indicator to the audience that we have officially moved on from any sort of technical accuracy. McTiernan held onto this language-switching technique after seeing it used in Stanley Kramer's 1961 courtroom drama, *Judgment at Nuremberg*.

He is doing this to tell us he knows. He knows these Russian military men would never speak to each other in English, but he is not as concerned with arbitrary accuracy as emotion. The actors could certainly speak to each other in Russian the entire time, but McTiernan's theory is that it would distract from the performances. On top of that, having actors from all over the globe memorize their detailed lines in another language would take far too long. The technique is also a callback to McTiernan's own learning experiences with foreign films, where he never read the dialogue in the subtitles. Instead, he watched the actors tell the story visually. If the opportunity to rid his film of subtitles presented itself, why not capitalize on it?

In fact, a great deal of *The Hunt for Red October* is John McTiernan

John McTiernan (left), Sam Neill (center), and Sean Connery discuss the opening scene of *The Hunt for Red October* (Paramount Pictures, 1990).

returning to those days spent at the AFI under the tutelage of Ján Kadár. This "action" film barely fits into its own genre because of its willingness to build tension with hardly any reliance on explosions or gunfire. Every young cadet in the background on these submarines, and every character directly involved with the central plot, has depth and wit, informing the entire frame with an intelligence that sets it apart from any sort of conventional action blockbuster. There are no real background players here, because everyone has a job to do.

One of the biggest techniques McTiernan employs in *Red October* is the moving cut he used a few times in *Predator* and more regularly in *Die Hard*, where one moving camera shot is cut directly into another. Even though it had been effective in *Die Hard*, the technique was still foreign to most American editors, so much so that McTiernan had to replace his editor in the middle of post-production to get the effect he wanted. The moving cut is, once again, an example of his European tutelage shining through, making *Red October* less a genre picture and more a bridge between what he had mastered in his two previous films.

The Hunt for Red October was another massive hit, both critically and commercially, for John McTiernan. Siskel and Ebert praised it, with Siskel pointing to "Baldwin's convincing, low-key approach to playing a film hero," and Ebert calling it skillfull [and] efficient."[5] Most of the major publications championed McTiernan's work. He had made the full transition from action filmmaker to, for lack of a better term, action *auteur*.

Red October was number one at the box office for three weeks in March of 1990, with its domestic gross coming in at just over $122 million against a $30 million budget.[6] The success of *Red October* also convinced Hollywood that Tom Clancy's novels were paperback cash machines; Clancy's Jack Ryan stories are still being adapted and continue to be recast; Clancy's brand is still solidified in popular culture to this day. Everything was looking up for John McTiernan once again, and from here he decided to go back into the jungle to test the limits of his dramatic storytelling abilities.

And he brought his *Red October* star with him.

13

There Will Never Be Another *Red October*

Even though John McTiernan had found global success with a pair of action pictures, in his third major feature film he was directing something entirely different than *Predator* or *Die Hard*. *The Hunt for Red October* looks like an action movie, it sounds like an action movie, but it is most certainly *not* an action movie. At least not in the traditional sense, and it is a type of film that will probably never see the light of day in Hollywood again.

The tension in *Red October* exists because of the patience with which it tells its story. Not a single gun is fired, there is maybe one legitimate explosion in the depths of the ocean, and there are no foot chases or big brawls between characters. In modern-day Hollywood, this approach would no longer work, not for a big-budget blockbuster saddled with specific box-office expectations and prepackaged through a marketing machine. For evidence, consider any of the submarine movies to come in the years and decade after McTiernan's film, and the general evolution of blockbuster filmmaking since 1990.

Jonathan Mostow's 2000 submarine thriller *U-571* was almost wall-to-wall action with a video-game aesthetic, a film that gets things kick-started with a torpedo blowing apart a submarine and scattering the crew across the ocean. There are moments of tension, but they are interspersed among torpedoes and fires and explosions. The 2002 Kathryn Bigelow thriller *K-19: The Widowmaker*, starring Harrison Ford, was based on a true story but still leaned heavily on kinetic action and adrenaline in the form of a race against time. Perhaps the closest bunkmate to *Red October* was the 1995 thriller *Crimson Tide*, Tony Scott's battle of wills between a tenacious submarine captain and his immediate subordinate. While *Crimson*

Tide also relied on the verbal fireworks between the two leads, Gene Hackman and Denzel Washington, it was still not entirely dedicated to hanging on to quiet tension, and steadily morphed into an action movie using visceral thrills as its tension currency; the third act of *Crimson Tide* becomes a story of mutiny and a guerrilla-style takeover, which lend themselves to action. The finale of *Red October* is about soldiers and men talking, discussing their situation, and finding a resolution; in other words, this is the way this sort of thing may actually happen.

Aside from the submarine subgenre, movies like *The Hunt for Red October* were pushed headlong into action for the next three decades. Thrillers needed explosions and car chases and gunfire. Even the Jack Ryan films, as the franchise changed hands from Harrison Ford to Ben Affleck to Chris Pine, pivoted away from the Tom Clancy model of exposition in order to intensify kinetics.

These days, Hollywood would be too nervous to allow a movie like *Red October* to unfold at such a deliberate pace. There would be unavoidable pressure from the studio executives to insert a torpedo battle, or a more visually intense deep-sea chase sequence than the one on display here. Action would need to be added to justify spending the sort of money on such an ambitious thriller.

The aforementioned Chris Pine reinforced this sentiment when he was doing press interviews for *Star Trek Beyond*, the third film in a reboot franchise in which he plays Captain James T. Kirk. *Star Trek Beyond*, like its predecessors, is primarily an action/chase film, drawing certain criticism from Trekkies who longed for the sort of deep-thinking, philosophical drama that was a staple of the original 1960s television series (and a substantial element of the better films).

As Pine said in an interview with *SFX* magazine, a cerebral *Star Trek* story "just wouldn't work in today's marketplace."[1] He went on to discuss the themes of his *Star Trek* films, and how even though there may be heavy existential questions in his films, they must be disguised by furious action set pieces and CGI.

That same observation cuts across all avenues of modern moviemaking, and it makes *The Hunt for Red October* feel like that much more of a relic. McTiernan may have had *Treasure Island* in mind when he took on the project, but his *Red October* also feels like a throwback to classic military dramas, cut from the same cloth as the 1957 Robert Mitchum adventure *The Enemy Below*, or Robert Wise's 1958 classic *Run Silent, Run Deep*.

Part IV: The Connery Years

Sean Connery (left), Alec Baldwin (center), and Scott Glenn in *The Hunt for Red October* (Paramount Pictures, 1990).

No longer would such a patient approach be allowed to breathe the way McTiernan's film does over the course of two-plus hours. Things would be tightened, explosions would be added, stakes would have to be raised visually in order for a studio like Paramount to sell their film to modern audiences whose attention spans have understandably shrunk over the last three decades. Media delivery systems are getting quicker, moving rapidly as attention is more fractured and less patient for an action picture that takes its time.

In a sense, modern technology and the day-to-day onslaught of information has helped to render a film like *Red October* obsolete.

14

Finding the *Medicine Man*

Following the trifecta of wildly successful and groundbreaking new action films, John McTiernan could write his own ticket in Hollywood. Paramount was eager to get the next two Jack Ryan films into production with McTiernan directing and Alec Baldwin back in the lead role.

But the next film in the series was going to be *Patriot Games*, Tom Clancy's Jack Ryan follow-up to *The Hunt for Red October*. It featured Ryan taking on the Irish Republican Army, specifically a rogue IRA terrorist seeking revenge on Ryan and his family. McTiernan and Baldwin are both of Irish-American ancestry, and they found the subject matter too sensitive to their personal lineage.[1] They passed on the opportunity to continue the franchise, and in stepped Phillip Noyce to direct *Patriot Games* with Harrison Ford taking over in the central role.

Ford would play Jack Ryan in both *Patriot Games* and the next film, *Clear and Present Danger*, before the franchise was handed over to Ben Affleck in *The Sum of All Fears* in 2002. After that film missed the mark critically and financially, another reboot was attempted, in 2014 with Chris Pine, in *Jack Ryan: Shadow Recruit*. Again, that attempt failed to get the Jack Ryan story back on its feet.

After passing on *Patriot Games*, McTiernan and his wife (and producing partner), Donna Dubrow, took advantage of the break in his schedule to purchase Bear Claw, a shabby 3,300-acre ranch outside the North Central Wyoming town of Sheridan. The country home nestled at the edge of the woods, and the painterly sky hanging over the rolling plains stirred McTiernan's soul. It was his reward for success. Having spent his formative years on a family farm in upstate New York, McTiernan had enough of an agricultural background to repair the faulty irrigation on the property and restore fields that had become overgrown and barren.

They also began breeding livestock in the form of Beefalo, a hybrid of American cattle and Bison.[2]

In the meantime, a bidding war had broken out in Hollywood over a new Tom Schulman screenplay. Schulman, who had won the Best Original Screenplay Academy Award for 1989's *Dead Poets Society* and had a pair of hit comedies under his belt with *Honey, I Shrunk the Kids* and *What About Bob?*, penned a new script called *The Stand*. It told the story of a doctor who finds a cure for cancer deep within the canopy of the Amazon rainforest, only to have the cure ripped from his hands due to a number of extenuating circumstances.

The screenplay was eventually renamed "The Last Days of Eden" and, ultimately, *Medicine Man*, and studios were anxious to grab the rights. Eventually, a new studio offshoot of Disney named Hollywood Pictures paid Schulman $3 million for the screenplay, and they began to put together a cast and crew for production.

John McTiernan and his *Red October* star, Sean Connery, were interested in bringing *Medicine Man* to the screen. Connery agreed to star, and had so much faith in the screenplay he came on board as executive producer. McTiernan was equally as excited to re-team with Connery as the two had a positive working relationship on the *Red October* set. McTiernan also saw this as another opportunity to reshape his directing career. He approached *Medicine Man* as if it were an art-house film, a decision that may have played a part in its cold reception.

McTiernan certainly did not let the troubles he had on the *Predator* shoot deter him from returning to the jungles of Mexico. This time, Veracruz would serve as a stand-in for the Amazon rainforest.

Connery's Dr. Robert Campbell was the focus of *Medicine Man*, but the female lead was crucial, and still needed to be cast. Dr. Rae Crane would serve as proxy for the audience, brought in as an assistant in the opening sequence to learn exactly what Dr. Campbell was up to in the jungle. Her character would also develop a tangential, almost cryptic romantic relationship with Campbell. It was a tricky balancing act.

McTiernan brought in Lorraine Bracco who, in the early stages of discussing the part, had acted in only a handful of films and television shows, the biggest being the role of Tom Berenger's wife in Ridley Scott's thriller *Someone to Watch Over Me*; but Bracco's star was considerably on the rise by the time McTiernan began filming.

Bracco had landed the role of Karen Hill, gangster Henry Hill's wife

14. Finding the Medicine Man

in Martin Scorsese's *Goodfellas* the year prior to *Medicine Man* filming. By the time they began the shoot in March of 1991, Bracco was enjoying a Supporting Actress Oscar nomination for the role. Unfortunately, she was going through a messy divorce with her husband, actor Harvey Keitel, at the time of the shoot, and she wasn't necessarily in the right frame of mind to head out to the jungle. Her nerves had been stretched thin, but she still jumped at the chance to act alongside Connery.[3]

Despite the jungle setting, the story of *Medicine Man* could not be any different than what McTiernan had done in *Predator*. There would be no special effects to speak of, only a humanistic tale of passion, obsession, and loss. The sets were, for the most part, rather static and easily manageable, save for a few key scenes where McTiernan and his crew had to rig up cranes for camera shots one hundred feet above the ground. It would be difficult, but by this time in his career McTiernan had juggled all manner of challenging terrain; a few shots high atop the Mexican jungle would be a walk in the park compared to some of his past endeavors.

Production ran from March to June of 1991, and post-production and marketing had the film set for a 1992 release. But Hollywood Pictures clearly did not have the sort of confidence in the film that they had when they paid Tom Schulman $3 million for the script, as it was handed an early February release date. February, as well as January and September, have often been labeled as the months on the calendar where studios dump films they have no confidence in and want to simply try and make the budget back. It was not the most promising sign.

Medicine Man did not find the sort of fanfare or positive buzz, or ultimately box-office numbers, of McTiernan's previous three films. It was not any sort of game changer, or really anything memorable beyond late-winter theater filler. Critical reception was lukewarm at best, and while it may have made its production budget back ($45 million against a $40 million budget), it wasn't the sort of thrilling adventure film audiences had grown accustomed to in McTiernan's work.[4]

It isn't that *Medicine Man* is a bad film, per se, it's just a mediocre one, which is surprising given McTiernan's track record. Connery delivers a strong performance as the eccentric doctor, and the sets and cinematography from Donald McAlpine (who also shot *Predator*) are at least competent. The problem, in most peoples' opinion, was Lorraine Bracco. Her Dr. Rae Crane is set up to be this specific fish-out-of-water character, and Bracco lands those early moments as she steps into this unfamiliar setting.

83

But her performance grows increasingly erratic and inconsistent as the plot unravels. Her character, as written in the screenplay, appears to be missing the necessary intellect to create a convincing scientist. Bracco winds up doing more of an imitation of Kate Capshaw's grating, damsel-in-distress character from *Indiana Jones and the Temple of Doom*. Her shrieking and aloofness work against the part, and steal any credibility from the role.

There is nothing particularly inventive about the *Medicine Man* screenplay to separate it from a dozen other films, which is odd given the bidding war that was attached to Tom Schulman's draft. The story has the eccentric doctor, the female assistant, and the two push against each other for a while before eventually falling in love, and so on and so forth. It was a familiar narrative, and it had just as much to do with the film not hitting expectations in 1992.

In the summer of 1992, *Medicine Man* saw a bit of a resurgence in the public eye when a doctor, Wilburn H. Ferguson, and his partner, Phillip Lambro, filed a lawsuit against Sean Connery, Tom Schulman, and their representative company, Creative Artists Agency (CAA), claiming they had stolen their story for the film.

Dr. Ferguson, a Texas physician, had researched jungle plants in the Amazon in the 1930s and '40s and allegedly developed a cure for cancer through said research. However, the American Cancer Society denied his funding and the research was eventually lost to the jungle. Ferguson turned the story of his research into a book, *Tsanza*, which was published in 1973. In 1988, Ferguson and Lambro took their book and their story to CAA to pitch a film adaptation. It was here that, according to Ferguson's lawsuit, Schulman and the creative forces at CAA took the idea and repackaged it, cutting Ferguson and Lambro out of the proceedings.

The lawsuit was eventually settled out of court.[5]

For whatever shortcomings *Medicine Man* has, it was not a cataclysmic misfire. Nor was the direction the biggest issue with the film. In fact, if anything worked it was the visual aesthetics, namely the incredible shots McTiernan and McAlpine managed to capture atop the rainforest canopy.

McTiernan's name still carried with it a certain air of respectability, and after *Medicine Man* came and went he was still one of the hottest filmmakers in Hollywood. It was clear he was ready to dive headfirst back into action filmmaking after pushing himself in different directions over the last two pictures. The problem turned out to be that the project on which he would eventually land would cause a shift in McTiernan's career. The project was big. Too big. And too ambitious. It would be McTiernan's first glimpse into how marketing and hype can ruin a film before a single second of celluloid has been captured.

And it would be the first sign of McTiernan's growing mistrust of the Hollywood Studio Machine.

Part V

Too Big to Fail?

15

Extremely Violent

Like so many twenty-three-year-old men in 1991, Zak Penn loved action movies. He spent a great deal of his adolescence and college years at Wesleyan University absorbing all the hits from Schwarzenegger, Stallone, and Norris. His friend and fellow Wesleyan University graduate, Adam Leff, held the same predilection for these sorts of fireball blockbusters.

In 1990, when Penn and Leff graduated from Wesleyan, they did what any young action-loving cinephiles would do, or at least what so many of them *wanted* to do: they wrote an action screenplay. Only their screenplay, while certainly paying homage to the films, was not just going to be another action movie full of explosions and car chases and one-liners, even though those were the films which inspired the duo; instead, this screenplay took a meta-fictional, deconstructionist approach to the stories they loved. They took what they knew from '80s action and began to endow it with sharp satire.

Their screenplay told (at least it eventually told) the story of a young boy who obsesses over action movies, namely those of his big-screen idol, Arno Slater. One night, a magic ticket sends the boy hurtling into the world of Slater, and the bulk of the story takes place in this action movie world of inconsequence and perfection. The films they loved served as their main inspiration, but Penn and Leff also found direction from the unlikely world of Woody Allen.

Allen's 1985 romantic fantasy *The Purple Rose of Cairo* is a story about a movie star (played by Jeff Daniels) who walks right off the screen and into the life of a down-on-her-luck waitress in Depression-era New Jersey. Penn and Leff would use the basic setup, only reverse course and have the character in *their* real world be transported cinema-side.

The working title for the screenplay was "Extremely Violent," and

Penn and Leff had no major ambitions about it when they finished the initial draft and decided to pick up an agent and peddle it around Hollywood. Their agent, Chris Moore, knew there was something here that would sell, and he pushed for it to find an audience somewhere in Tinseltown. Much to the surprise of these two wide-eyed scribes, the "Extremely Violent" screenplay caught the attention of the right people in Hollywood; rumors abounded, and a bidding war broke out over the rights. Columbia Pictures eventually won the bidding war for $350,000, an incredible haul for two unproven Hollywood rookies.

If that wasn't enough to delight Penn and Leff, a certain hulking megastar had laid eyes on their work and wanted to play the lead: Arnold Schwarzenegger himself.

The irony of Schwarzenegger's involvement in the picture was the character in Penn and Leff's screenplay—cheekily named Arno Slater—was a sendup of the type of action star Schwarzenegger had made his millions playing for more than a decade. Despite Schwarzenegger loving the idea of the script, he had some issues with the screenplay's namesake: the extreme violence.

In 1991, about the time Schwarzenegger read through the screenplay, he was enjoying the fruits of his latest blockbuster hit, James Cameron's game-changing science-fiction sequel, *Terminator 2: Judgment Day*. This follow-up to Cameron and Schwarzenegger's 1984 action-thriller had dominated the summer box office in 1991, spending a month at number one and doubling its budget with over $200 million in ticket sales.[1] It had also permanently altered the face of blockbuster filmmaking, having fully incorporated the use of Computer Generated Imagery, or CGI, technology to create a villain made of liquid metal. Cameron used CGI technology for a few scenes in his 1989 deep-sea adventure *The Abyss*, but in *Terminator 2* he created an effects revolution in Hollywood.

But *Terminator 2* was also a violent film, warranting a hard R-rating. Perhaps that is why Arnold Schwarzenegger was a little concerned about the violence of Penn and Leff's screenplay; maybe he wanted a change of pace. That would be a possible explanation as to why Schwarzenegger was going back and forth between the "Extremely Violent" screenplay and a film called *Sweet Tooth*, in which he would play the Tooth Fairy.

The executives at Columbia were pressing Schwarzenegger, however, and they eventually talked him into starring in the untried screenwriters' vehicle. But Schwarzenegger requested that professional writers come in

15. Extremely Violent

to fix the screenplay. Just like that, Zak Penn and Adam Leff were subtly pushed out of center frame. They were paid handsomely for their story, and in came Shane Black and his partner, David Arnott.

Since 1987, after appearing alongside Schwarzenegger in *Predator* and gaining a substantial bit of notoriety with the success of *Lethal Weapon*, Shane Black had been busy defining his own action voice in Hollywood. *Lethal Weapon* had gotten its first of three sequels in 1989 (Black was credited with the story), and his screenplay for *The Last Boy Scout*—formerly named "Die Hard" until Joel Silver negotiated the use of that title—had become a solid hit for Warner Bros. in 1991.

Black and David Arnott, who had written the screenplay for Andrew Dice Clay's lone venture into action moviemaking, 1990's *The Adventures of Ford Fairlane*, were tasked with injecting some energy and muscle into the "Extremely Violent" screenplay. Penn and Leff's story was much more subdued and deliberate in its pacing when compared to what wound up on the screen; Columbia had visions of big summer blockbuster dollars clouding their mind. They wanted setups and payoffs to come fast and furious, so they put together something that worked for the executives, who then handed everything over to John McTiernan.

The McTiernan hiring surprised Penn and Leff, who were now on the outside looking in on their story as it was quickly turning into something they could no longer recognize. They felt McTiernan was too serious and pragmatic an action filmmaker to do the satire in the story any justice; but, again, they no longer had a say on the fate of their story. Shane Black and David Arnott were also surprised when they discovered McTiernan wanted to make substantial changes to their work.

McTiernan renamed the film "Last Action Hero," which stuck; but the rest of his edits were met with resistance from Black and Arnott. Tempers were flaring and eventually Black and Arnott were fired from the project. The screenplay would then go on an increasingly troubling journey through the hands of a few mercenary script doctors until it became a bloated, tonally manic mess.

First, the screenplay was sent from McTiernan to William Goldman, Academy Award–winning screenwriter of such classic films as *Butch Cassidy and the Sundance Kid*, *Marathon Man*, and *The Princess Bride*, to try and fix issues that had only metastasized after passing through five writers. Goldman was a legend, and he was paid as such; Columbia executives handed him a check for $1 million.

After Goldman, a handful of other writers took their own shots at *Last Action Hero*. Larry Ferguson, who had just gone through ground-floor rewrites with McTiernan on *The Hunt for Red October*, made his own additions to the story. At one point, even Carrie Fisher was brought in to add a woman's touch. With every hand-off and addition and subtraction, the screenplay was chopped up with certain ideas left in and others taken out. That meant some of McTiernan's specific additions were in there right next to William Goldman's, which were then mixed in with Larry Ferguson's and Carrie Fisher's, and the confluence of ideas and tones and direction was overflowing.

The revisions continued on until the screenplay became a Frankensteinian behemoth of a dozen different visions all crammed into one incoherent narrative. But the studio executives at Columbia were not as concerned with the patchwork screenplay, because they had secured Arnold Schwarzenegger and they had given him a $15 million paycheck to headline the movie. That is all movies needed to bring in a mint at the box office, or so it seemed.

It was the arrogance of Columbia that ultimately doomed the film. Right after Columbia brought McTiernan on board to direct, studio head Mark Canton pumped up *Last Action Hero* in every avenue of mass marketing he could think of before a single reel of footage had been captured. Video games, action figures, and a soundtrack full of original songs from some of rock's biggest acts at the time were pre-packaged. And, worst of all, the release date was set, come hell or high water, for June 18, 1993.

There was a big problem with that release date, a problem roughly 65 million years in the making. A week before the release date, on June 11, Steven Spielberg was set to release his adaptation of the Michael Crichton bestseller *Jurassic Park* on the world. While *Hook* had been a rare flop for Spielberg in 1991, this adaptation looked to be anything but a disaster. It was predisposed to be the movie of the summer, the hype was already building, but Canton and Columbia figured they had plenty of ammunition to fend off Spielberg's dinosaur movie. They were the ones who had the immovable object to combat Spielberg's unstoppable force. They had an Austrian superstar.

But they also needed to find someone to play the kid, Danny Madigan, opposite Schwarzenegger. Austin O'Brien, who had just gotten his career started with a handful of commercials and a small role in the 1992 science-fiction horror *The Lawnmower Man*, was brought in and spent a few days on set with Schwarzenegger before he was eventually hired. The rest of the cast was an impressive collection of serious actors like Anthony Quinn, Ian McKellan, and F. Murray Abraham, and a wide swath of terrific character actors like Charles Dance, Art Carney, Tom Noonan, and Robert Prosky. Mercedes Ruehl, fresh off her Supporting Actress Oscar win for 1991's *The Fisher King*, was hired to play Danny's mother, Irene. The cast was inspiring, but when filming began in August 1992, just about every other element of the production had its wheels shot off at one point or another.

If the preproduction troubles weren't enough of a red flag, the chaos that ensued on set, which was handled by the studio with a lethal combination of ignorance and bravado, began hammering nails into the proverbial coffin.

Schwarzenegger was proving to be a bit of a headache on set. Perhaps it was his ego, or his lack of confidence in the film, but whatever the case he was difficult early and often. Schwarzenegger would bicker over the sort of boots Jack Slater would wear and spent days test-driving cars before finally deciding on the one he wanted Slater to drive: a gold 1969 Pontiac Bonneville convertible. The liberties Schwarzenegger was taking with everyone else's time created tension between he and McTiernan. Besides that, McTiernan was starting to realize the scope of this film and the trouble it was in.

One afternoon, Shane Black and David Arnott visited the set. An executive with Columbia allegedly told the writing duo to pay a visit to Schwarzenegger, who was taking a break in his trailer. McTiernan saw the interaction, and it was enough to convince him that Black and the studio were going behind his back to either sabotage the film or take it away. Relationships became icy. Black left the set and didn't return.

Meanwhile, the budget continued to swell. At the time, a $60 million invoice on a summer action movie was a substantial number—these days, $60 million is the sort of price tag applied to mid-level independent dramas released in limited theaters around awards season. Sets were lavish and expansive and a few caused logistical nightmares. The La Brea tar pits, for example, had to be recreated for one scene where Jack Slater falls off a skyscraper and into the tar. The gag is, once he leaves the pit covered in tar it takes a few small napkins and he is squeaky clean; back to normal. The expense outweighed the payoff, which became the status quo.

McTiernan could see the writing on the wall grow bolder and cut deeper every passing day. One of the more fundamental problems plaguing the entire production was the tone of the story; executives were trying to shape this into their own movie, and they could not decide if it was going to be a relatable, safe kid's movie or a satirical action/thriller trying to get the attention of the older, teenaged crowd.

As the shoot dragged on for five months, McTiernan was growing increasingly weary and just looking at the finish line instead of directing the film in front of him. When it comes to film shoots, McTiernan had always aimed for an eighty-day shoot from start to finish. *Last Action Hero* ran 141 days.[2]

Workdays topped out at eighteen hours, but even that was not enough time to hit the editing room more than three weeks before June 18, where even more problems surfaced. McTiernan and his team worked to cobble together a coherent vision and a consistent thematic through-line; but, with elements of Penn's screenplay, Black's revisions, Arnott's additions, Goldman and Fisher, et cetera, all converging into an incoherent and tonally inept mess, there was no easy way to convincingly glue the pieces together. That is why the picture has madcap inconsistencies. For example, an animated cat detective named Whiskers, voiced by Danny DeVito, played a pivotal role in the film. And he was featured in the same movie as Tom Noonan's terrifying child murderer, who kills our hero's son in the first act. One moment strictly for children; another, decidedly not.

Even when some gags should have worked in the film, edits made explanations and punch lines disappear. Transitions from one sequence to the next were slipshod as the editors patched things together.

And still, all of these headaches didn't stop the marketing campaign, which was still spiraling out of control in much the same way as the film itself, into levels of insanity. At one point, the studio paid half a million dollars to put the film's title on the side of a NASA rocket that was subsequently launched into space, where nobody would see the banner.

Then there was the issue of a seventy-five-foot inflatable Arnold Schwarzenegger, as Jack Slater, holding sticks of dynamite in one hand and a sawed-off shotgun in the other, erected in Times Square mere months after the February 1993 bombing of the World Trade Center. It didn't take long for the studio to recognize this offensive, if innocently shortsighted, gesture, and remove it under the cover of night. But these inflatables were scattered across a few different locales in the U.S., only now with the stigma of poor taste attached.

15. Extremely Violent

McTiernan was in over his head, drowning in film stock while the publicity machine churned along, soullessly shilling for an unfinished project. Murmurs indicated that the film was on life-support, but Columbia remained steadfast and were determined to take on Spielberg in the summer.

The premiere for *Last Action Hero* should have been a joyous celebration of a summer action-spectacle, featuring the planet's biggest superstar. But word had been steadily leaking out regarding the trouble on set, the infighting, and the ballooning budget. Negative press hung over the film's premiere like the albatross of a forgone conclusion.

In its opening weekend, *Last Action Hero* pulled in just over $15 million, landing in the second place spot behind *Jurassic Park*, which more than doubled McTiernan's movie with over $38 million in its second weekend. *Jurassic Park* was rolling on its way to over $400 million domestically. *Last Action Hero* fell to number four behind *Jurassic Park*, *Sleepless in Seattle*, and the big-screen adaptation of *Dennis the Menace* in its second week.

John McTiernan (left), Arnold Schwarzenegger (in driver's seat), and young Austin O'Brien (in passenger seat) discuss an early chase sequence in *Last Action Hero* (Columbia Pictures, 1993).

The thirteen-week run in multiplexes ended with a thud, and an embarrassingly low $137 million worldwide box-office take—only $50 million of that final tally was made up of ticket sales in the United States.[3] Adding insult to injury, *Jurassic Park* ended its theatrical run with almost four times *Last Action Hero*'s haul. It was the biggest disaster of McTiernan's and Schwarzenegger's respective careers up to that point, and it left executives at Columbia with their tails tucked between their legs. It was the sort of epic misfire that sent ripples across the industry, and it reshaped the way Columbia did business for a few years until they were out from underneath the debt of *Last Action Hero*.

16

Last Action Hero: Ahead of Its Time or Timeless Disaster?

Time and nostalgia can do interesting things to movies. Sometimes, it reinforces an initial reaction; other times it can give a movie a second chance. Perspective is constantly shifting, and what was once seen as a masterpiece can lose some of its luster with the passing of years, becoming something mediocre in the court of public opinion. On the other hand, derided films shoveled on the embers of past Hollywood fires can find new life, new love, and the much-sought-after "cult" status too many films lay claim to in this era of the endless nostalgia parade.

Somewhere in this abyss of reconsideration lies *Last Action Hero*.

"Ahead of its time" is an easy footnote to attach to *Last Action Hero* because of its meta-fictional structure. It's the moniker most regularly attached to dense, thoughtful science-fiction movies, or stories with clever structural techniques, or pictures with high concepts and even higher aspirations. Calling a movie ahead of its time is the dismissive shorthand for telling someone they simply did not understand what the film was trying to say, and *Last Action Hero* eventually became a film "ahead of its time" in the collective mind of some fans.

The notion of breaking apart popular genres in a way that is a bit more intellectually complex than simple spoofs—like the *Airplane!* movies or *The Naked Gun* franchise—seems like a perfect nostalgia-driven idea from the 2010s, where what used to be in the zeitgeist is being brought back through a lens of more careful introspection. The themes of *Last Action Hero* are, for lack of a better term, quite brilliant: A young boy being raised almost entirely on action films, with a hard-working but absent mother and no father figure, gets transported into the world of his favorite franchise and goes on an adventure with his action idol, using his knowledge of this fantasy world to stay ahead of every character in the movie. In 1993, this was a fresh perspective on the action genre that had grown to prominence in the fifteen years prior. Action movies were never bigger than they were in the 1980s, thanks in no small part to John McTiernan. Even though Zak Penn and Adam Leff were surprised by McTiernan's hiring, having a prominent action director send up his own genre should have been the stroke of genius it looked like on paper. But ideas can only carry a film so far; eventually, the execution has to match the ambition. That's where McTiernan's satirical deconstruction absolutely collapses.

Last Action Hero spins out of control with the energy and brainpower of its half-dozen screenwriters spilling out across the screen with reckless abandon. One scene doesn't fit with the scene before it, and it is a mismatch with the scene after. Tones shift relentlessly, jokes fall flat, and eventual tedium sets in; the film grows increasingly at war with itself over its two-plus hours.

First of all, this is a movie that's supposed to be aimed at pre-teens. At least that was the intended demographic when all the dust settled on the rewrites. This is a story for boys like the one in the film, Danny Madigan; boys who, in 1993, admired everything Arnold Schwarzenegger did on the screen. Yet, despite its intended audience, *Last Action Hero* has some incredibly dark, problematic elements that have no place within the walls of a whimsical, PG-13 deconstructionist action-comedy.

The tonal issues begin with a rooftop sequence in the cinematic world of *Jack Slater III*, the movie sequel *inside* the movie. Tom Noonan's unsettling serial killer, The Ripper, clad in a yellow slicker and sporting a face that belongs among the undead, winds up killing Slater's young son by pulling him off said rooftop. This is some heavy material for a movie that, in no short order, will begin mocking the entire existence of these characters and throwing every sight gag imaginable at the screen in the hopes that some of it sticks. Very little of it does.

The "real world" portions of *Last Action Hero* are drab and unforgiving, which might make sense. It is intended to juxtapose the glossy cinematic language that painted the Slater universe. This world is a miserable place for Danny, making his eventual foray into the movies all the more rewarding for him. Only McTiernan and the platoon of credited writers take things too far in this real world.

16. Last Action Hero

A drug addict breaks into Danny's apartment, assaults him, and handcuffs him to the radiator in the bathroom. This is a harrowing sequence, completely unwarranted and entirely too realistic. It may be emphasizing the bleakness of Danny's real life, but this is a scene from the dour, rain-soaked reality that takes the gloom too far.

Once Danny does wind up in the backseat of Slater's car inside the movie screen, the next hour or so is spent in this absurdist movie setting. But things aren't as fun as they should be, mostly because this extended sequence takes the rapid-fire approach, filling the story with jokes stacked on top of jokes, and a cavalcade of split-second cameos from famous actors that serve as nothing but a distraction. It winds up being the bulk of the film, and a great missed opportunity. If the shooting script had any semblance of a definitive, consistent approach to the material, a faux reality inside an action movie could have been loaded with the right kind of sharp satire and perfect comedy beats. But, with so many cooks adding their own ingredients, this world founders.

The tone stays light for the most part in Slater's world, and McTiernan

John McTiernan and the crew shoot the fake premiere of *Jack Slater IV* in Times Square in *Last Action Hero* (Columbia Pictures, 1993).

effectively shifts the palette from a rain-soaked and dour New York to an overlit and hopeful Los Angeles. Almost all of Schwarzenegger's lines feel like one-liners, shot out as rapidly as the weightless gunfire. A henchman is killed with an ice-cream cone, Slater's car appears to almost fly in certain shots, and physical scenery shifts wildly to indicate this is all being filmed on a stage somewhere.

The entire story inside the movie world is off balance. There is the introduction of that cartoon cat detective. It is nothing more than a pandering gimmick tossed in from one of the dozens of rewrites, and while it may be an attempt to send up the falsity of this world by including an animated character, it is most certainly not a clever indictment of the action genre. That was the intention from the beginning, but that intention was lost once Whiskers the cat made his debut.

For the sake of argument, let's agree that these movie-world scenes do manage to capture the romanticized aesthetic of a twelve-year old boy like Danny. But that also misses the intention of these scenes. They are supposed to be an actual fake world inside the real one, not simply an imagined projection from Danny. And besides, even if that was the intention, the editing is a mess and there is no indicator that this is a proper reading of the material.

Certain establishing scenes are missing; other scenes are cut short; the pacing is frenetic. This choppy editing should at least make for a brisk midsection, but it somehow works in reverse. The cuts are too manic, creating a stop-and-start narrative that never gets an honest opportunity to breathe or find any sort of real flow, and the story stumbles upward through the visuals while the endless stunts and gags grow tiresome. This is a thirty-minute story somehow crammed into an hour, and the monotony is crushing.

Just when the jokes reach peak ineffectiveness, we are back in the most unforgiving portrait of real-world Manhattan since Scorsese and De Niro showed us the hate-filled hell of Travis Bickle in *Taxi Driver*. And this is in a kid's movie, no less. Slater and Danny have to follow Benedict (Charles Dance, arguably the brightest star in the entire film), the central villain, back through the movie screen and into this dreary reality. Slater finds out the hard way that punching out windows and crashing cars hurt here. If the abrupt visual shift to a taxing reality like present-day New York wasn't enough, Benedict decides to test out the violence, and its subsequent lack of police presence, by murdering a civilian for literally no reason. This, like the opening scene, is needlessly violent and mean-spirited; it has no place in a movie like *Last Action Hero*.

While the tone continues its manic roller-coaster ride, we are privy to a third act that feels as endless as the second, where endings stack on top of each other, and any sharp satirical opportunities are completely dissolved beneath a tiresome, relentlessly long film.

For example, there is a scene where Slater and Danny must save the "real" Arnold Schwarzenegger at the premiere of *Jack Slater IV*. This scenario could have been a gold mine. Slater meeting Schwarzenegger is rich with possibilities, but here it winds up being nothing more than a throwaway sequence where the two meet each other and little to nothing happens. At one point, the screenplay had Slater meeting Schwarzenegger, who drones on and on about his Planet Hollywood restaurant chain. For whatever reason, that gag was scrapped and replaced with nothing. It is a sad, rushed moment, clearly edited after the fact, made all the more shocking by the film's insistence on running other jokes into the ground.

There is no reason why *Last Action Hero* should run north of two hours. As a lean ninety- to 105-minute satire, it might have had a chance. But the bloat, like the gangster with explosives inexplicably stuffed into his distended belly at his own funeral in the Slater universe, weighs everything down and kills any momentum. In one of the three or four false endings, Death, played by Ian McKellan, steps out of a screening of what is supposed to be Ingmar Bergman's *The Seventh Seal* and visits Danny and a dying Jack Slater as they try desperately to get Slater back into the movie.[1] He informs Danny he isn't there for either of them, and divulges a quick tip to move the story along: find the other half of the magical movie ticket.

What's the point of this sequence at all? For starters, the intended audience for *Last Action Hero* would have no connection of any kind to *The Seventh Seal*, an existential Swedish film almost forty years old in the early 1990s. Beyond that, Danny could have remembered to find the ticket in the theater lobby on his own, possibly trimming five to ten pointless minutes from the movie. It would have helped, but it would not have been enough.

Last Action Hero may have been conceptually ahead of its time, but that does not excuse the finished product. With seemingly dozens of screenwriters, all with their own ideas inserted into the story, frenetic editing, and one reel too many, nostalgia is not enough to save this film.

And critics were not on board with McTiernan's vision either, savaging the film and only adding to the negative buzz surrounding the premiere.

High concept must still be executed with confidence and a uniform goal between the creators and the money. It is not enough to have the concept if the studio executives spend an inordinate amount of time undermining the creative process.

Last Action Hero proved disastrous for McTiernan and everyone involved. Especially the studio, which was being crushed by *Jurassic Park* at the box office week after week. McTiernan knew everything had been rushed in order to meet a deadline, and the project from start to finish was about a month too short to truly allow things to fall in place and have more time in the editing room. Thankfully, in all this mess, McTiernan and Shane Black managed to amend their relationship after sharing in the misery of the film's failures.

According to Shane Black in the Nick De Symlian article at *Empire*, one night, after the film had been out for a while and subsequently slipped out of cultural consciousness, McTiernan joined Black and Schwarzenegger for a drink and a little reminiscing.[2] McTiernan was still proud of the movie, despite all its flaws. Whatever the case, he was ready to move on as quickly as possible, and the prospect of a new *Die Hard* adventure had caught his attention over at 20th Century–Fox.

Hollywood has an interesting way of redeeming its fallen heroes. Sometimes it never happens after a movie as disastrous as *Last Action Hero*. Michael Cimino fell into obscurity after *Heaven's Gate*. Rob Reiner never fully recovered after his disastrous family comedy *North*. Most of the time, however, for people this talented, the next hit is just around the corner. Schwarzenegger rebounded almost immediately, teaming up once again with James Cameron for his high-flying spy adventure *True Lies* in 1994, leaving *Last Action Hero* behind as a rare misstep. Shane Black would continue writing action screenplays, the next of which was *The Long Kiss Goodnight*, a thriller starring Geena Davis and directed by Renny Harlin.

As for Zak Penn, he would continue to build a career of hits and misses. After *Last Action Hero* he wrote a pair of comedies, *PCU* and *Inspector Gadget*, and the action script *Behind Enemy Lines*. Finally, the biggest break in his career came a decade after *Last Action Hero* when he crafted the story for 2002's *X-Men* sequel, *X2*. The superhero film was a hit with critics and audiences, and it set up Penn in Hollywood for the foreseeable future. His partner on *Last Action Hero*, Adam Leff, eventually found success as a columnist for *Vanity Fair* magazine.

McTiernan would almost immediately find comfort in the arms of a familiar character, and he would get back to basics to find his voice as a filmmaker once again.

He would be back, with a vengeance.

17

"Simon Says"

Jonathan Hensleigh was just getting started in Hollywood in the early 1990s. He wrote the screenplay for a small Disney movie, *A Far Off Place*, and penned a handful of episodes for *The Young Indiana Jones Chronicles*. While he was working on those episodes to pay the bills, Hensleigh also put together a screenplay for an action thriller called "Simon Says." The screenplay took him just eleven days to write, but selling the story took quite a bit longer.

The motivation for the story had come to him when he remembered an incident from when he was ten years old. While playing outside, Hensleigh accidentally hit another kid in the face with a rock. The kid suffered only a few minor injuries with no long-term effects, but the memory sparked an idea that festered in his mind all the way to these early years in Hollywood: What if that kid had suffered life-altering injuries and, corrupted by a burning desire for revenge, sought to ruin Hensleigh's life as an adult?

From that idea spawned the story of a New York police officer, in his mid-thirties, being systematically tortured by a madman—an adversary from the officer's past—who is threatening to destroy the city unless the officer jumps through his elaborate hoops; the city is basically transformed into an obstacle course. A few studios sniffed around "Simon Says," including Warner Bros. who, at one point, fashioned the story as a *Lethal Weapon* sequel. But New York City was a key component of the screenplay, and Martin Riggs and Roger Murtaugh had always been Los Angeles cops. Without a place for "Simon Says," Warner Bros. pushed the screenplay back out and 20th Century–Fox bought it. They had different plans for the story; while the nuts and bolts of the script would remain intact, the studio wanted Hensleigh to re-fashion the characters to fit into a *Die Hard* sequel.

17. "Simon Says"

Hensleigh agreed, but he found the process arduous. He was having a hard time reworking his story to fit the continuing adventures of John McClane. In fact, he was having such a tough time that Fox was close to firing him and bringing in the dreaded script doctors to rearrange things. In a desperate move, Hensleigh took his script to John McTiernan, who was aching to get back on his horse after the *Last Action Hero* debacle. 20th Century–Fox jumped at the chance to have McTiernan back in the *Die Hard* franchise, so the two got to work on "Simon Says" to try and retrofit it into the world of John McClane.

The first hour of the shooting script remained Hensleigh's "Simon Says" screenplay almost verbatim. Hensleigh and McTiernan shaped the rest of the story around the John McClane character, and during the brainstorming sessions Hensleigh came up with the idea to make this *Die Hard* story more of a direct sequel to the original than a continuation of the second film. And his idea would let him keep the original inspiration for his screenplay intact.

What if this Simon was, in fact, the disgruntled brother of Hans Gruber, Alan Rickman's villain from the 1988 film? What if Simon Gruber was so eaten up with rage and bloodlust he decided to torture his brother's killer? McTiernan was sold on the idea, and "Simon Says" began to evolve into *Die Hard: With a Vengeance*.

But Simon Gruber's desire for vengeance was a little too basic to carry a feature film. The revenge story actually needed to be a subplot, and another story needed to take center stage. A heist made perfect sense, given the lineage of their villain. Hensleigh thought first of an art heist, but the idea of a sociopathic European criminal and his crew carrying around canvas paintings felt a little too dainty. There was no heft to an art heist.

Then, Hensleigh remembered reading an article in the *New York Times* about America's gold storage. Despite the common conception that most of the country's gold bullion supply was in Fort Knox, Kentucky, the majority of it actually resided below the streets of the New York Stock Exchange. Simon and his team stealing truckloads of gold was a substantial physical heist, and it opened up the story for several action set piece opportunities. Hensleigh began crafting the third-act heist around truckloads of bullion being swiped from the bowels of the Stock Exchange and carried to a ship waiting in the harbor.[1]

Hensleigh's detailed descriptions and intricate knowledge of the underground storage was so accurate that the FBI felt he was worthy of investigation. He had to assure agents that he had gotten all of this detailed information from that *New York Times* article, and they accepted his citation.

McTiernan handed over Hensleigh's screenplay to Bruce Willis, who had been busy looking for the right *Die Hard* screenplay and rejecting everything he had been given up to this point. One of the prospective screenplays was called "Troubleshooter," which involved a terrorist takeover of a cruise ship. *Die Hard* on a boat, basically. But Willis felt it was too similar to the recent Steven Seagal hit, *Under Siege*, so he turned it down and kept looking.[2]

Since he last played the John McClane character in the 1990 sequel directed by Renny Harlin, Willis had been struggling to find his footing, and stumbled from one cinematic misfire to another. Right after *Die Hard 2*, Willis did the voice work for his uninspired comedy sequel, *Look Who's Talking Too*, and played journalist Peter Fallow in Brian De Palma's disastrous adaptation of Tom Wolfe's *Bonfire of the Vanities*. He followed these duds with a trio of confounding films: the drab thriller *Mortal Thoughts*, the universally derided caper comedy *Hudson Hawk*, and a small role in the awful gangster film *Billy Bathgate*.

Thanks to the help of Shane Black and director Tony Scott, Willis had another hit in 1991, playing a burned-out private detective in the hit action film *The Last Boy Scout*. From there, Willis flexed his comedic muscles in Robert Zemeckis's *Death Becomes Her*, and eventually found his way to the set of Quentin Tarantino's game-changing masterpiece, *Pulp Fiction*, where he played the double-crossing boxer Butch Coolidge. Even though he had scattered a few more forgettable thrillers around *Pulp Fiction*, Tarantino's film was such a seismic shift in Hollywood that it revived Willis's career, resuscitated the failing career of John Travolta, and turned Samuel L. Jackson into a star.

Nineteen ninety-four felt like a good time for Willis to step back in the shoes of John McClane, but the script had to be right. He read Hensleigh's work and felt it was a terrific setup and a natural place for the evolution of the character.

With McTiernan and Willis on board, the project got the green light; but there was still casting work to be done before they could begin filming. McClane had a partner in *Die Hard: With a Vengeance*, a more involved, active partner than Reginald VelJohnson's Sergeant Al Powell in the original. This time, the partner would be a Harlem shopkeeper who would bail out McClane early on, then be reluctantly swept up in the action. Samuel L. Jackson made perfect sense in the role.

When initial discussions between Jackson and the *Die Hard* team began, *Pulp Fiction* had just blown away audiences at the Cannes Film Festival, and word was beginning to seep out. Before his turn as the philosophical hit man Jules Winfield in *Pulp Fiction*, Jackson had been one of the hardest working character actors in Hollywood, amassing a substantial portfolio that included bit parts in *Coming to America, Do the Right Thing, Goodfellas*, and *True Romance*. Jackson's hardened energy and fierce edge fit perfectly for Zeus, the ardent Harlem shopkeeper who regrets his intervention almost immediately. Even though Willis and Jackson shared no scenes in *Pulp Fiction*, they had become friends during production and the chemistry they built with one another carried over to the shoot in New York.

As for Simon Gruber, McTiernan needed an actor cut from the same cloth as Alan Rickman in the original film. They sent the screenplay to British actor Jeremy Irons, who had been a force in Hollywood for years, having already won a Best Actor Academy Award in 1991 for his work in *Reversal of Fortune*. Irons was a fan of McTiernan's work, so it took very little to convince him to come on board.

There was also the small issue of Simon, and the way he was portrayed in Hensleigh's original script. Since it was initially the story of a man who was wronged as a child and seeking revenge, Hensleigh went to the local book store and picked up all the Mother Goose books to craft a rhyming, riddling dialogue for Simon. It didn't make as much sense in the new context of a John McClane story, but McTiernan loved the playful dialogue. And he was confident Irons could execute the rhyme wordplay competently, so all the riddles were left in place.

Die Hard: With a Vengeance presented an entirely new series of challenges for McTiernan, who had never filmed on location in New York City. He was able to work around some of the logistical nightmares by moving interior shots to the boroughs outside Manhattan. But the bulk of the action takes place right on the island. Rather than having some nearby city like Toronto or Cleveland stand in for Manhattan, McTiernan leaned into the city's iconic settings and made sure to use as much of the real locations as humanly possible. That meant blocking off large sections of the city at any given time, which created seas of onlookers and cars honking at the sight of Bruce Willis. Traffic was a nightmare anywhere McTiernan and his team set up shop.

The opening sequence took place in Harlem, and McTiernan was worried that the infamous sandwich board Simon makes McClane wear—with bold, red letters spelling out "I Hate Ni**ers" scribbled across the front—would stir up the community and possibly cause violence from anyone who did not realize what was happening. Which was understandable. The sign could also be the target of paparazzi, who were always close by ready to snap a photo of Willis; having a shot of him in a sandwich board with hate speech painted across it would have been a tough thing to explain. To avoid any issues, McTiernan had the words added in post-production, and aside from one clear shot of those CGI words the camera held on tight shots of Willis's head and shoulders to avoid the red script and allow McTiernan to get the shots he needed.

Die Hard: With a Vengeance was going to be, much like the previous two John McClance adventures, all about the action set pieces. The only difference this time around was that the story did not take place in one location. With the first film inside Nakatomi Tower and the second film taking place entirely in Dulles Airport in Washington, D.C., building sets and having more control over the environment was an easier task. This time, the entirety of New York City was going to be the canvas, and set pieces would be inserted in real settings. Manhattan would become a character in and of itself, and McTiernan managed to pull off some impressive sequences thanks to the cooperation from city officials.

One of the action sequences involved a taxicab, which McClane and Zeus commandeer, racing across blocks of traffic jams and, at one point, directly through the lawn of Central Park. This sort of extended, dangerous stunt could have easily been filmed in a less-populated city, like Cleveland, or in a smaller park that would be easier to control. A great deal of it could have taken place on a sound stage with the city added in post-production. But McTiernan always knew the importance of authenticity, so he put in the time and effort to execute these grand moments in the places they belonged.

The cab really does race through busy city streets in Manhattan, weaving in and out of traffic, except actors have a difficult time concentrating on driving and performing for the camera. McTiernan had a control booth mounted on the back of the cab. The booth, which looked like a small dune buggy cockpit extending from the trunk, would have the real controls

17. "Simon Says"

to the cab and a stunt driver would control it. That way, Willis and Jackson could deliver their lines without having to avoid traffic, and being able to avoid crashing into another car.

When the chase sequence heads into Central Park, these rousing moments are shot inside the actual park with stunt performers and extras dodging the taxi as it zigs and zags from one side to the other. The finale of this scene has McClane clearing a wall in Central Park and launching the cab out on to a busy city street. Amazingly, the scene all happened the way it is shown in the movie, and it all took place on location.

The cab sequence leads right into another complex sequence for McTiernan, only this time sets and façades would be required. It was the subway explosion scene, where a bomb sends a subway car careening across a platform under Wall Street, causing an explosion on the street level and creating a gaping hole in the ground. For this, McTiernan and Fox had to purchase an empty lot in the middle of Manhattan and create a false courtyard area with an entrance into the subway. The subway platform was built specifically for the film. Actual subway cars were purchased, but their insides were removed and replaced with V8 General Motors' engines so stunt coordinators could control the cars and direct them where they needed to go. It was a complicated bit of filmmaking, but the moment was executed to perfection and the end result turned out to be worth the difficult setup.

Near the end of the second act, John McTiernan made a rather sizeable visual departure from his typically grounded, literal form of action storytelling. The scene involved McClane riding atop a dump truck, which was being propelled through an aqueduct by water from an exploded dam. McClane would, for lack of a better term, "surf" on the truck before grabbing hold of a dangling grate and being shot through a tube, out of the duct and into the air.

All laws of physics discounted just about everything in this scene, and on top of that McClane was going to be shot into the air at the exact time Jackson's Zeus character was driving by; they were the sort of logical hang-ups McTiernan would not have been able to look past in his earlier films, but this was a new day and McTiernan came into the job with gusto, and a point to prove. He was having fun during the shoot, and he knew more coincidences and absurdities were on the way, so he embraced them instead of trying to work around them.

Even though he knew the water would appear phony when it was

Part V: Too Big to Fail?

added in postproduction, they rigged up the dump truck and went for it. The scene was not a home run—the water, like McTiernan predicted, looked too absurd to fully sell the scene—but it at least captured the adventurous spirit of McTiernan's intentions.

As the shoot reached the latter portion of the story, McTiernan and Hensleigh found themselves struggling to nail down an ending. The original ending had McTiernan and Zeus escaping the ship just as it explodes, which is in the final cut; only in this first rendition, Simon and his band of thieves are aboard the ship when it explodes. The end.

This ending was eventually vetoed, but nothing substantive was put in its place.

One problem McTiernan and Hensleigh had with the direction of the climax was that it put John McClane on a ship out in the middle of the ocean, miles away from the bomb Simon said was planted in a New York school. It was stealing the hero from the real action, but it was too late to correct course that drastically; McClane was here, on this boat. Now what?

John McTiernan (forefront, wearing cap), Samuel L. Jackson (upper right, partially obscured), and Bruce Willis (far right) discuss the bridge scene from the end of *Die Hard: With a Vengeance* (20th Century–Fox, 1995).

17. "Simon Says"

They came around to the idea of making the bomb in the school a hoax, therein placing the actual bomb on the ship. While it cleared up the issue of McClane's misappropriation, it felt like one twist too many for McTiernan. But again, he went with it, and it put the wheels of the current ending in motion. Now, the finale would involve Simon and his team faking their own deaths and escaping, which was Hans Gruber's intention in *Die Hard* before McClane ruined that plan; this twist at least had some symmetry with the original film.

There were two endings filmed for *Die Hard: With a Vengeance*. One featured Simon escaping, which didn't feel right in the John McClane universe. The other, which became the theatrical ending, had McClane tracking Simon across the border into Canada and taking down his helicopter. It was a messy end, and a messy route to said end, but it all managed to come together, for better or worse. The shoot wrapped in December of 1994, and the release date was set for May 19, 1995.

Critics were lukewarm on *Die Hard: With a Vengeance* when it unofficially kicked off the summer movie season in 1995. Ebert mildly praised it. Some critics enjoyed the Rube Goldberg–style plot machinations; others found Samuel L. Jackson to be a welcome addition to the franchise. But regardless of critical praise or disdain, the John McClane franchise had reached a point where it was critical Teflon. Analysts could have mercilessly hammered the movie and it still would have opened well and had some legs at the box office. Having McTiernan back in the driver's seat was icing on the cake, so to speak. *Vengeance* wasn't too big to fail, it was too "John McClane" to fail.

The box office proved as much. *Die Hard: With a Vengeance* grabbed just over $22 million in its first weekend on its way to a $100 million domestic haul. That was enough to cover the $90 million budget, and the additional $266 million foreign take solidified the film's overall success.[3] However you slice it, *Die Hard: With a Vengeance* was a much-needed hit for McTiernan and Bruce Willis.

In the bitter wake of *Last Action Hero*, here was John McTiernan the filmmaker returning to the franchise that made him, and managing to create a fresh new adventure while simultaneously bringing the John McClane story back to its roots.

18

No McTiernan, No Real McClane

It would be twelve years after the release of *Die Hard: With a Vengeance* before John McClane would grace the screen in another sequel. In 2007's *Live Free or Die Hard*, McClane and Holly have finally ended their tempestuous marriage; McClane is living the bachelor cop life and judging from the brief domestic scenes he seems to be at least a passable co-parent, looking after his grown-up daughter who becomes a hostage as the plot unfolds. This story in question revolves around cyber-terrorists—a plot point as indicative of the year as anything. The early 2000s were a popular place for behind-the-scenes cyber villains in the movies. Beyond the story and the setting—in and around Washington, D.C.—and the brand of villain, sat an almost unrecognizable John McClane.

The John McClane in Len Wiseman's film is not the same person audiences came to love in the first three films. To go even further, the John McClane that popular culture has engrained in its collective consciousness exists in only two films. And it just so happens, the two most interesting and complex iterations of McClane are in *Die Hard* and *Die Hard: With a Vengeance*, the only two films in the franchise with John McTiernan behind the camera.

McTiernan and McClane—or, more accurately, Bruce Willis—seem to share a true understanding of what makes the John McClane character tick. He is not just a good cop in the wrong place at the wrong time; he thrives on adversity and he is at his best when he is pushing back against evil to defend the domestic life he's crafted for himself, and the life of the citizens around him.

Only two films place John and Holly at odds. In Renny Harlin's *Die Hard 2*, John and Holly have made up since the original and they are happily in

18. No McTiernan, No Real McClane

love when terrorists seize control of the airport. In *Live Free or Die Hard*, the two have come to terms with their marriage. They are divorced, but the split doesn't seem contentious. Even if it is, their relationship barely matters in the fourth film.

Having John and Holly at odds further indemnifies the audience with McClane, because it emphasizes the content of his character. This terrific police officer can save hostages, or rescue a city, but he can't seem to keep his home life in order no matter what he does or how hard he tries. Or perhaps he isn't trying hard enough.

The fourth and fifth *Die Hard* films attempt to replace the marital strife with paternal tensions, but it does not land the same way. In *Live Free or Die Hard*, McClane has to save his precocious daughter, Lucy, but their relationship is never given the depth of Holly and John in the first film (even in *Vengeance*, although Bonnie Bedelia does not appear in the film, their crumbling marriage is an underlying problem from the opening scene).

The same can be said with the unconvincingly strained father/son dynamic at the center of *A Good Day to Die Hard*, but the fifth film is a disaster on countless fronts; the relationship between John and his son, played by Jai Courtney, is one issue of several.

The last two *Die Hard* films also manage to take the bulk of John McClane's instinct out of the story, leaving them with a reactionary pinball action hero and not a fully realized human being. Part of what made McClane so endearing and identifiable in the first film was the fact that he frequently used his intuition and quick thinking. It was his brain that got him off the exploding rooftop, and it was creativity that helped him foil Hans Gruber with the Christmas tape. He did not rely solely on his brawn or his durability to get in and out of predicaments, which is precisely what he does in *Live Free or Die Hard*, *A Good Day to Die Hard* and, to an extent, *Die Hard 2*.

Of the other three sequels, *Die Hard 2* comes closest to capturing the essence of the McClane character. In Harlin's film, Willis still has the physique of a normal person, and his methods are anything but flawless. His inability to save the doomed aircraft on the snowy runway humanized the character, and it felt at least like a logical continuation of the person we met in McTiernan's original. But, again, there is no conflict in McClane's life to intensify the stakes, and his initial involvement with the terrorists is all wrong. He uses a paper-thin hunch to investigate the two terrorists who sneak into baggage claim, thrusting himself into the action rather than having the action come to him.

This raises another major issue with the franchise outside of McTiernan's involvement; too often in those other films, McClane is forcing himself on the plot. The curious snooping at the airport, the willingness to pick up a computer-hacking kid in danger in the fourth, and traveling to Russia to specifically rescue his son in the fifth are all proactive decisions from McClane. He is a man with whom deliberate reluctance and the desire for inaction better serve the story. He is left without a choice in the original film, and in *With a Vengeance* it is a vendetta forcing him to shake off his hangover and get to work. These stories are what have always defined the real John McClane as a reluctant hero.

When *A Good Day to Die Hard* hit theaters in February of 2013, it was clear the John McClane who helped change the face of action genre back in 1988 was no longer available. In his place was a disinterested Bruce Willis, shuffling through a ridiculous plot. Now, in *A Good Day to Die Hard*, McClane punches a civilian in the face, shuns his son's need for affection, and falls through floors of a building engulfed in flames.

To compare this to the desperate man who, in the original *Die Hard*, is pulling glass from his bleeding feet and telling a man he has never met face-to-face to tell Holly what she means to him if he doesn't survive this ordeal, may be the clearest indication that the franchise had lost track of its hero. McClane has now become an overcooked macho jerk who tells his son they don't hug.

The last two entries in the franchise should never have happened, at least without collaboration from McTiernan. The way *Die Hard: With a Vengeance* served as a perfect bookend to the original, with Renny Harlin's exciting (albeit slight) second film sandwiched in between, the "original" three adventures of John McClane fit together with the precision of a Swiss watch. Considering the latter two pictures in the canon, the symmetry of McClane's story is thrown askew in mediocre to less-than-mediocre fare.

Nobody understood John McClane quite like John McTiernan, which is why of the five films in this franchise, the first and third are the ones which truly manage to capture the essence of the cinematic hero we continue to admire today.

PART VI

Highs and Lows

19
Trouble at Home

John McTiernan may have repaired his beaten and bruised directorial reputation with the success of *Die Hard: With a Vengeance*. The film served as a palette cleanser following the forgettable *Medicine Man* and the calamitous *Last Action Hero*. But in the months and years following *Die Hard: With a Vengeance*, McTiernan's personal life found more than enough turmoil.

It started with a conflict back on his Bear Claw ranch in Northern Wyoming. When McTiernan and Donna Dubrow moved into the sprawling 3,300-acre ranch in 1991, they immediately began repairs and renovations on the property. Some of their renovations involved installing new irrigation systems to boost crops and water their herd of Beefalo. McTiernan tapped into Smith Creek, which ran from the nearby Bighorn Mountains, and by the letter of the law it was his right to use said rivulet for his irrigation plans.

Wyoming water rights work in a first-come-first-served basis, and McTiernan and Dubrow's ranch was number four on that list in the region. The number-three rights belonged to their faraway neighbor, Sam Scott, who allegedly had not used the water for his land in over five years; since the water was not in use, McTiernan and Dubrow began using the number-three rights to further advance their irrigation systems.

But in 1996, Scott moved back onto his property and planned to use his water to irrigate a series of smaller ranches; these smaller, divided properties would then be parlayed into homes for sale. McTiernan immediately filed for abandonment against Scott, a move that legally bound him to the number-three rights as Scott had been away for more than five years.

While the maneuver may have been legal, abandonment is a filing rarely upheld in court. Sam Scott claimed he had been using the water for

Part VI: Highs and Lows

John McTiernan (right) and Bruce Willis take a break on the *Die Hard: With a Vengeance* (20th Century–Fox, 1995) set.

irrigation the entire time, and decided to take McTiernan to court over the issue. McTiernan was not buying Scott's assertion, however. In fact, he was so certain that Scott had not been using the water he paid for seven NASA satellite images of Scott's property to prove it. The cost of these images: $2,500 each.[1]

Around the same time McTiernan and Scott were battling over irrigation tracts in Wyoming, McTiernan's marriage to Donna Dubrow began to unravel. The increasingly contentious relationship was being soured by, among other things, what may have been McTiernan's increasing paranoia with the studio system in Hollywood. He blamed meddling studio executives for the failure of *Last Action Hero*, and his distrust with just about everyone around him was intensifying. Whatever the case, in 1997 McTiernan and Dubrow separated and shortly thereafter McTiernan filed for divorce.

The divorce proceedings would grow even more querulous over the better part of the next decade, and it would intensify once revelations regarding McTiernan's investigative techniques surfaced.

20

The Norse Debacle

John McTiernan's separation from Donna Dubrow may have inspired him to try something entirely new as a director. He had gotten wind of a Michael Crichton novel heading into production: *Eaters of the Dead*. This was the opportunity he had been searching for, to try his hand at the horror genre with the help of major studio dollars in his corner. The goodwill he had re-established with *Die Hard: With a Vengeance* was enough to instill confidence in Touchstone Pictures, who owned the motion picture rights to *Eaters of the Dead*.

Then again, several of McTiernan's films were big-studio projects; and much like *Last Action Hero*, *Eaters of the Dead* would prove to be another studio-meddling debacle, resulting in yet another low point in the director's career.

Chicago native Michael Crichton was a global phenomenon by the late '90s. As the previous decade belonged to the fiction of Tom Clancy, the 1990s were a landscape dominated by the heady science-fiction thrillers from Crichton. He had been a prolific novelist since the late '60s, and in 1973 he made his first mark in Hollywood directing *Westworld*, the story of a fantasy theme park for wealthy adults where the robot exhibits there begin turning on those same rich tourists. It would be that very theme in his 1990 novel, *Jurassic Park*, that would make him a household name.

As successful as Crichton's *Jurassic Park* was, the Steven Spielberg film adaptation in 1993 captured the imagination of the world and pushed the story's influence even further.[1] It also made the back catalogue of Crichton's novels some of the hottest properties in Hollywood, and adaptations of his current publications were almost a foregone conclusion. Following *Jurassic Park* were adaptations of his 1992 Japanese thriller *Rising*

Sun; his 1994 male sexual-harassment drama, *Disclosure*, set against the backdrop of the Seattle tech boom; the messy adventure film *Congo*, based on his 1980 novel *The Lost World: Jurassic Park*; and the psychological science-fiction thriller *Sphere*, which he had penned in 1987.

While most of these vehicles were moderately successful at the box office, none had anywhere near the cultural impact as *Jurassic Park*, which is understandable. Even though adaptations like *Congo* or *Sphere* had not been major hits, and neither were well-received critically, Crichton's work was still in demand in 1997, and *Eaters of the Dead* would be the earliest of his works to find its way to the Hollywood adaptation factory.

Published in 1976, *Eaters of the Dead* is Crichton's loose novelization of the *Beowulf* myth. It tells the story of an exiled Arab who teams up with a group of Vikings to fight off impending evil. Crichton was on board as a producer, a job he had also taken on with the adaptations of *Disclosure* and *Sphere*. McTiernan and Ned Dowd also joined as producers, and their original plan was to keep the book's title intact and lean into the horror elements that made the novel such a compelling read.

It was going to be McTiernan's first foray into the horror genre, but test audiences—too often the deciding factor when it comes to a director's vision—would change things significantly.

There was no marketable Arabic actor in Hollywood to take on the central role of Ahmad ibn Fadlan, the court poet of Baghdad who is exiled and eventually takes up with the band of Norsemen. Touchstone Pictures needed to sell tickets more than they needed to stay culturally appropriate, but they still made the wise decision to not do something problematic, like change the nationality of Ahmad and fill the role with a popular white movie star. Instead, they split the difference, and recruited Antonio Banderas for the role.

Banderas, born in Málaga, Spain, was an established leading man by 1997. After getting his start in Spanish-language films during the 1980s, Banderas broke through Stateside as Nestor Castillo in Arne Glimcher's 1992 musical biopic *The Mambo Kings*. From there, he grabbed a supporting role in Jonathan Demme's *Philadelphia* playing the lover of Tom Hanks's condemned lawyer, and soon turned his attention to the action genre in films like *Desperado*, *Assassins*, and *The Mask of Zorro*. The dashing Banderas had a rogue's flair for adventure and a smoldering intensity, and McTiernan would push him to curb some of his confidence in order to play a meek court poet in the early scenes.

20. The Norse Debacle

By the time Banderas signed on to "Eaters of the Dead," he was commanding an average salary of $8 million per picture. The rest of the central cast would save money, populated by relatively unknown actors whose physical stature and size would be just as important as their performance. All except one.

Having Omar Sharif agree to play a small role as Melchisidek, Ahmad's traveling partner through the first act of the film, was a major step towards credibility for the movie. Sharif was a legend in 1997, having appeared alongside Peter O'Toole in David Lean's 1962 classic *Lawrence of Arabia*, and having starred as the title character in Lean's 1965 epic *Doctor Zhivago*. Sharif was excited to appear in a Viking horror film like the one McTiernan had in mind, and would be one of the most disappointed members of the cast when things turned out the way they did.

The Vikings needed to be large, imposing, and they needed to be able to dwarf Banderas's five-foot-nine-inch frame in the early scenes. McTiernan and his team of producers searched far and wide for the right actors, eventually landing on athlete-turned-actor Vladimir Kulich to play the leader, Buliwyf. The rest of the team was filled out in short order, and in June of 1997 the cast and crew headed north to the forests of British Columbia, Canada, to begin filming.

McTiernan battled through the elements like a seasoned professional. The terrain was wet and cold and unforgiving, but McTiernan had experience in the hottest of Mexican jungles; he shot scenes atop rainforest canopies; he filmed inside the cramped confines of a submarine; he captured a car pursuit through Central Park in New York City during daytime hours. A little rain and colder temps were no trouble for him. The trouble came in the form of studio executives.

Touchstone Pictures was the mature branch of Walt Disney Studios; it began in 1984 and promptly dove into producing darker, more serious films targeted at adult audiences. Over the next decade, Touchstone produced some of the most popular films in Hollywood, from *Good Morning, Vietnam*, to *Pretty Woman*, to '90s action-blockbusters like *Con Air* and *Armageddon*. In 1997, the confidence they had in their business model coupled with the clout they carried in the industry meant they had more say than McTiernan when it came to the finished product.

But they weren't so sure what to do with this one. McTiernan wanted horror, which Touchstone was fine with, but it needed to be PG-13 so it would be marketable (and saleable) to the largest audience possible. He may have had some reservations, but McTiernan decided the rating was not a deal breaker, so he and his editor John Wright made sure to deliver what Touchstone wanted.[2]

He finished the rough cut of the film with "Eaters of the Dead" still the working title. McTiernan was also steadfast in sticking to the Arabic themes, having the music stay regionally appropriate, and the demonic horror at the core of Crichton's story was still prevalent. There was even an early trailer to accompany the rough cut. This original teaser is ominous, featuring hordes of torch-bearing warriors traveling across hills shrouded with fog, lit in a hellish red hue. There are flashes of beasts, and Antonio Banderas's silhouette can be seen after the title card. It is an impressive minute-long glimpse into McTiernan's singular vision.

Test audiences hated the rough cut. Vehemently. Reactions were overwhelmingly negative, sending Touchstone execs into full-on damage control. They approached McTiernan to fix certain elements of the story that did not play well, most notably the Middle-Eastern influence. Executives decided they needed McTiernan to pull back on the fact that Ahmad was Arabic, despite his blatantly Arabic name and geographical background. This also meant cutting out the Arabic score, which had been fully completed by Graeme Revell by the time the test screening happened. Things would only get worse.

Another major issue the studio (and, perhaps more importantly, the test audience) had with McTiernan's rough cut was that it was *too* scary. In a truly maddening bit of double talk, the studio said they needed certain elements of the story to be softened, but at the same time they needed some guts and gore added to get the rating back up to an R. Never mind that McTiernan had shot the entire film with a PG-13 rating in mind; he would have shot the entire film differently had he planned on making it R-rated.

Touchstone also wanted to soften the title so as not to scare away any prospective ticket buyers. The softening of some elements and the enhancement of others made the entire process a confusing amalgamation of mixed messages. Touchstone's image of the story was not heavy on the horror, but reliant on action and violence. "Eaters of the Dead" was too intense, too horrific, so the title was changed to *The 13th Warrior*. In the meantime, Oscar-winning composer Jerry Goldsmith was brought in to re-score the entire picture.[3]

The back and forth with executives became too much for McTiernan,

20. The Norse Debacle

who began doing re-shoots; but he did so while pushing back against the increasingly ridiculous demands. The extensive re-shoots also forced Touchstone to move the release date back several months from the prime real estate of summer 1998, to the less certain land of spring 1999.

Disaster was percolating.

Sensing the possibility that McTiernan was going to abandon the project, Touchstone brought in Michael Crichton to do his own set of re-shoots. Crichton and the studio went so far as to completely recast the role of Wendol's mother, the villain in the film, replacing seventy-two-year-old actress Susan Willis with a twenty-nine-year-old model and actress named Kristen Cloke. Originally, Wendol's mother (named Grendel in the original *Beowulf* story) was the central villain and was killed in the original climax. That changed with the hiring of Cloke, who took the character in an entirely different, mythical direction with the help of Crichton and the studio.[4]

Meanwhile, here was McTiernan, in one of the more bizarre studio catfights, doing his own set of re-shoots at the same time. They both knew what the other was doing, but neither would back down from their respective directorial duties. At one point during this mess, the cast and crew would shoot one entire sequence of the film for Crichton, then move to another studio on the same Touchstone lot and shoot the same section of the movie for McTiernan. It was an embarrassing bit of undercutting for many members of the cast, the majority of whom were new to the industry and under the impression that it would be their big break in Hollywood.

These bumbling, mismanaged re-shoots were what sent the budget skyrocketing, from the neighborhood of $85 million to north of $115 million. Eventually, McTiernan grew tired of the dueling studio shoots and left the project, leaving Crichton to finish the film as an uncredited director. The budget was rumored to have hit $160 million (with marketing and insurance claims and everything that goes into making a movie, these numbers are difficult to nail down to any specific dollar amount) and all was seemingly lost. Even if the film could fix half of its problems, news was beginning to steadily leak out regarding the troubled shoot. By 1999, bad buzz was enough to damage a movie's bottom line. It had only been four years since Kevin Costner's *Waterworld* redefined the way these troubled productions were covered in the media. The ill winds blowing around *The 13th Warrior* were like chum in the water to journalists.

Once the re-shoots concluded, the film had been pushed back a few

Antonio Banderas (left), John McTiernan (center), and Vladimir Kulich work through a scene on the set of *The 13th Warrior* (Touchstone Pictures, 1999).

more months, to August 27, 1999. While it was still technically a summer release date, the last weekend in August is typically relegated to dreck; children are returning to school, and fall activities are starting. This date, like the ones in January, February, and September, is often where studios will dump films in which they are less than confident.

In this case, Touchstone was right to lack confidence in *The 13th Warrior*. Critics approached the film with their torches already ablaze, no doubt having been lit by the rumors of production problems. *The Sixth Sense*, three weeks into its release, dominated at the box office, and *The 13th Warrior*'s final domestic tally limped in at $32 million. The global number: $61,698,899, about $100 million shy of the final budget.[5]

It was yet another hard lesson for John McTiernan regarding studio interference, in this case spoiling what could have been his first foray into the horror genre. Another seed was planted in the director's brain, and from this and the disastrous *Last Action Hero* shoot, the poisonous flowers of paranoia were beginning to sprout even more.

There is a great bit of irony when it comes to the messy *13th Warrior* debacle. That same month in 1999, one of the films that would outperform *The 13th Warrior* at the box office was a movie directed by John McTiernan.

21

In Defense of *The 13th Warrior*

    Films about Vikings are among the least represented in Hollywood; the mythos has never caught on with modern audiences as much as the tales of pirates and cowboys have done through the years. Of those scant films dealing with Vikings, none work better than *The 13th Warrior*.

    That being said, McTiernan's film has its fair share of issues, though none of them are bad enough to ruin the finished product. The storytelling is fractured and often flat, and far too many scenes are shot in an impenetrable shroud of darkness—probably to compensate for the weak CGI in the late '90s. And the narrative goes nowhere far too often; but to simply throw this film on the compost heap of films that were destroyed by their production issues is an unfair assessment. Holding this up next to other disasters of the time, Kevin Costner's infamous *Waterworld*, for example, is a disservice to what works. It may be faint praise, but this is better than *Waterworld*.

    There are ample redeeming qualities in *The 13th Warrior*, and despite the fact that Michael Crichton made sweeping changes in his re-shoots, most of the stronger sections of the film feel like the product of McTiernan's distinct directing style and his ability to capture beautiful images amid the chaos and carnage of a hectic story. There are some striking visuals here, clearly the work of John McTiernan, and certain scenes echo the greatness in his earlier work. There is no way to fully deduce what is his work and what is Crichton's, but much of the final product has McTiernan's fingerprints.

    There is an early scene, for example, where Antonio Banderas's Ahmad, who has teamed up with the band of Norsemen, has been trying to learn their language. Just like McTiernan did in *The Hunt for Red October*, he has a scene where Ahmad and the Vikings sync up their dialogue in English to eschew subtitles and focus on the action. It works just as well here as it does in *Red October*, only the film that follows is a bit clumsier and too often misses its tonal marks.

McTiernan wanted horror, and Arab influence, and those things are noticeably neutered here. The dead eaters attacking these Norsemen are almost entirely nondescript, creating little to no honest threat for our heroes. These horned silhouettes and shadowy beasts create no suspense, despite the fact that suspense is the very element this film needs from the opening frame in order to succeed.

It is unclear why McTiernan felt he needed a heavier Arab angle for Ahmad, or how it would have enhanced the film. In the middle of the second act, Ahmad prays to Allah during a rainstorm. We know from the outset that Ahmad is Arabic, mostly because he hails from that region of the world; enough said. The story moves on to other ethnicities and geographical regions, and leaning into Ahmad's Arab background would not fit in with the direction of the story. But, again, maybe it made sense in McTiernan's original vision that we will never see; and it would have been interesting to hear what Graeme Revell's score would have sounded like behind the visuals.

What is arguably most telling about the finished product is the run time. Typically, the length of a movie should not be an issue one way or another. A ninety-minute film can be just as magnificent as a three-hour film, and vice versa. Only when terms like "troubled production" creep into the external narrative of a movie prior to its release does the run time become a factor. *The 13th Warrior* clocks in at 103 minutes. It's an innocuous time in just about every scenario, except here.

This is a film combining the classic tale of *Beowulf* with the journals of the real Ahmad ibn Fadlan, who *did* travel to the world of the Vikings in the tenth century.[1] It is a globetrotting adventure, a story of supernatural beasts and foreign invaders and warriors coming together to fight off evil and death, and seek deliverance. It is the sort of cinematic adventure that deserves epic scope and story. A film like *The 13th Warrior* would be better served had it been expanded to at least two hours, probably more, where this fascinating medieval world could be expanded upon and showcased. In early drafts and cuts of the film, there is no doubt McTiernan's film was much longer and more expansive than the final theatrical version. Settling on 103 minutes with a film like this is what happens when studios panic and begin trimming scenes to get down to the bare bones of a story, because the number of showings in a theater becomes more important than the quality of the film once things begin to go south.

And so *The 13th Warrior* was stripped down to its bare necessities. The scale of a film about an Arab exile joining forces with Vikings to fight a horde of supernatural villains should overwhelm us; it does not. Instead, it is a tale confined to economical length, and one where little to no effort is spent on fleshing out anyone in the cast beyond the three or four central characters. But, at the same time, the action set pieces are effective.

The moments of relentless action are undoubtedly McTiernan's contribution. He handles these scenes with confidence and an attention for spatial geography, much like he did in *Predator, Die Hard*, and *Die Hard: With a Vengeance*. Action directing is McTiernan's greatest strength as a filmmaker, and it is one of the few elements that redeem *The 13th Warrior*.

Even though re-shoots and dueling directors crushed the confidence of certain actors on set, their collective performances in the film remain strong. As the leader of the Norsemen, Vladimir Kulich is an undeniable presence on the screen, the perfect foil for Banderas, who begins the adventure as a fragile poet and ends a fighter. Speaking of Antonio Banderas, the Spaniard was at the height of his action-star status in 1999; he is able to carry this film through all its missteps with a confident, ultimately heroic turn as the central character.

It's a shame we will never get to see McTiernan's original cut of the film. It might not be any better, but it could be. There is enough in this final cut of *The 13th Warrior* to see how the movie could have worked, and worked well, had McTiernan been given the latitude to make the movie he wanted from the beginning. And the teaser for his version is a captivating sixty seconds.

But studio executives and test audiences had, once again, interfered with John McTiernan's vision. With the failure of *The 13th Warrior* and the calamitous production of *Last Action Hero* now on his ledger, McTiernan's growing mistrust of the Hollywood business model was warranted, and studio confidence in his work was waning at the same time. Before long, this same mistrust would become his undoing.

22

Silver Lining

McTiernan left the disaster of *The 13th Warrior* behind. The exit allowed him to hop back on board a project that he had passed on previously. It was a chance for him to direct something a little different, and it would reunite him with Pierce Brosnan, the star of his feature debut, *Nomads*.

This would be a remake, the first of McTiernan's career, but it was clear the director had something in mind to make his version of the film stand on its own. In the process, he would not only direct a vivacious, energetic caper film; he would, for the first time in his career, explore a steamy sexual relationship between his two leads. What's more, their relationship would stand out from the demographically skewed hordes of cinematic romantic relationships that have been the status quo in Hollywood for ages.

Norman Jewison, born in 1926 in Toronto, Ontario, had begun his career in infant stages of television, directing several variety show episodes and television movies before getting his chance at feature filmmaking in his mid-thirties with the effervescent Tony Curtis comedy *40 Pounds of Trouble*. There was no turning back for Jewison, who went on to build an impressive career of critical and commercial success; the earliest great film in his decades-spanning run was the 1967 Best Picture winner *In The Heat of the Night*, a gritty look at racism in Southern, small-town law enforcement. The film earned Rod Steiger a Best Actor Academy Award as the hostile Mississippi police chief, Gillespie, and was a powerful examination of racial tensions that still existed like a long-standing hangover from the Civil War. Immediately after tackling that heavy material, Jewison turned his attention to a New York caper film with two of the era's biggest stars.

The Thomas Crown Affair was an original screenplay by a Boston-based attorney and part-time writer named Alan Trustman. It told the story of a rich, dashingly handsome bank executive who pulls off a complicated heist and imagines he's made a clean getaway. Except there is a prickly, young, female insurance investigator who is not convinced of his innocence, and as her investigation pulls her into his opulent world, the two begin to fall in love (or, more aptly, in lust).

The Alpha male superstar actor of the 1960s was Steve McQueen, who stepped into the eponymous role of Thomas Crown. Born in March of 1930, McQueen grew up in the unstable world of the Indiana reform-school systems before eventually making his way from the Midwest to California in his youth. He landed his first starring role in the 1958 B-grade science-fiction classic *The Blob*, and two years later he outshone Yul Brynner in *The Magnificent Seven*. Then, in 1963, he headed an ensemble cast in the World War II adventure film *The Great Escape*. McQueen was cultivating a career as the ruggedly handsome leading man; playing a suave millionaire like Crown was a chance for him to step out of his rough-and-tumble persona to show his charm was not solely based on rugged machismo.

Cast opposite McQueen was a young actress named Faye Dunaway, who had not yet become one of the biggest stars in Hollywood. Before this film, Dunaway had only appeared as part of an ensemble in a pair of small features before landing the role of Bonnie Parker in Arthur Penn's *Bonnie and Clyde*.

Though it is widely considered to be a classic American film as well as one of the catalysts for the industry change that blossomed in the New Hollywood of the 1970s, *Bonnie and Clyde* had a tough time finding an audience when it first hit theaters. It was shoveled around the country in limited release, playing at late-night drive-ins, and destined to come and go as a failure. That is, until film critic Pauline Kael praised the film in her *New Yorker* review. Kael's glowing analysis of Penn's film was the boost *Bonnie and Clyde* needed to gain traction, build momentum, and ultimately nab a staggering ten Academy Award nominations; this included the first of three nominations for Dunaway over the next decade. By the time she was cast as insurance investigator Vicki Anderson in Jewison's picture, and when the film opened in the summer of 1968, Dunaway's star was on the rise.

The original *Thomas Crown Affair* is a product of its time, a static, detached mixture of breezy indifference and wit, combined with some visually middling caper sequences. Depending on whom you ask, it was either an average entry into Steve McQueen and Faye Dunaway's respective catalogues, or a classic of the caper subgenre. Whatever the case may be, Jewison's film was a decent hit, but it was a disposable bit of theater—summer movie releases were not quite the same in 1968, roughly a decade before *Jaws* showed studios what could be accomplished in the hotter months of the calendar.

Pierce Brosnan had been a fan of *The Thomas Crown Affair* since he saw it as a fifteen-year-old. It was one of the films that shaped his early movie consciousness, and when he began to find success in the acting business he kept the notion of a *Thomas Crown* remake tucked away in his mind. He and his longtime producer friend Beau St. Clair had batted the idea back and forth for several years, but they were both busy with other projects. Brosnan, in fact, was preoccupied with playing James Bond.

After *Nomads*, Brosnan ended his run on *Remington Steele* and dedicated his career primarily to movie acting. He stayed busy through the 1980s in television movies before gaining at least a hint of notoriety in the 1992 science-fiction thriller *The Lawnmower Man*. In 1995, MGM was ready to change direction from Timothy Dalton's take on James Bond. He was too serious, too morose for the era, and they needed the wry confidence and sexual energy back in the role. They were aiming to make the series fun again, and it was clear Brosnan was a perfect fit for a 1990s James Bond when he debuted in 1995's *Goldeneye*. After his second stint as Bond in 1997's *Tomorrow Never Dies*, Brosnan saw an opening.

It was here that Brosnan and St. Clair's schedules lined up, and they received an updated screenplay from writers Leslie Dixon and Kurt Wimmer. Brosnan and St. Clair took the screenplay to MGM, who owned the rights to the original film, and they all reached the same conclusion when they decided on whom they wanted to direct: John McTiernan.

McTiernan also admired Jewison's picture, and he was not particularly interested in telling the same story again. But he read the screenplay in one sitting and realized this was, tonally, a different version from what Jewison had crafted. This would not be a remake as much as it would be a continuation, or distant cousin, to the original. The skeleton of Jewison's film was intact, but the story filled out the picture in an entirely different manner.

At the time of the original film's release, Steve McQueen was thirty-eight. Faye Dunaway was twenty-seven. When filming began on the remake in October of 1998, Pierce Brosnan had just turned forty-six. Now came

22. Silver Lining

the task of finding the right female lead to confidently hold her own against Brosnan's cheeky charm.

The only requirement McTiernan had of his female insurance-investigator lead, this time named Catherine Banning, was that she be equally as charming as Brosnan. The audience needed to be able to fall in love with her just as easily as they were able to side with Brosnan's Crown. A handful of actresses came and went in casting discussions before McTiernan and St. Clair settled on Rene Russo.

By 1997, after more than two decades of fits and starts as a model and actress, Rene Russo, a native of Burbank, California, had found her groove in a string of supporting roles in successful films. Her feature debut came when she was thirty-five in the 1989 hit baseball comedy *Major League*, in which she played the romantic interest of Tom Berenger's aging catcher, Jake Taylor. In 1992, she showcased athleticism as an Internal Affairs detective and romantic interest of Mel Gibson in *Lethal Weapon 3*; she carried her prickly feminist charm into *In the Line of Fire*, where she verbally sparred with Cling Eastwood; in 1998, she embodied maternal resolve as a desperate mother in Ron Howard's kidnapping thriller, *Ransom*.

Russo fit right in with the sort of character McTiernan wanted Catherine Banning to be, an independent woman, beautiful and tough. And there was one element of Russo being cast that McTiernan did not take into consideration, or even recognize, an element that would transform the role and its place in popular culture: Rene Russo was forty-five years old.

The fact that Russo was a peer of Brosnan, not an actress ten or fifteen years his junior, and the fact that her casting and subsequent interpretation was a groundbreaking moment in 1999 probably speaks more to the troubling, underlying sexism in Hollywood than it does to Russo's performance. Studios had always skewed younger when it came to their male leads' romantic interests; in the hands of another director, the Banning character could have been twenty-seven, maybe younger. Here, however, Russo's age would wholly change the complexion of the film for the better.

Aside from Brosnan and Russo in the lead roles, a third key character needed a face: Michael McCann, the New York detective investigating the heist. The role (named Eddy Malone and played by Paul Burke in the original) had to be in stark contrast to both Brosnan's Crown, a playboy executive who floats above the ground when he walks, and Russo's Catherine Banning, a powerful, sexually independent female. McCann is beaten down by his home life, immersed in his job, a dry cynic, and is barely able to mask his jealousy as he witnesses the sparks fly between Banning and Crown.

McTiernan approached Denis Leary for the part. Though he had gotten his start in stand-up comedy and delivering rapid-fire monologues for MTV commercials, Leary's delivery and the sardonic aggressiveness in his material also made him an alluring dramatic presence in a handful of '90s movies. He did his fair share of comedies during his run in the decade, including the *Lethal Weapon* spoof *Loaded Weapon 1* and the underrated Christmas comedy *The Ref*. But Leary's choices began consistently leaning towards drama, and he became the go-to actor for bellicose supporting characters and antagonists in films like *Wag the Dog* and *Suicide Kings*. His homespun cynicism made sense for the role of Michael McCann.

McTiernan kicked off his *Thomas Crown* adaptation with a wink at the original, casting Faye Dunaway as Crown's psychiatrist. It was a way for him to pay homage to the original while simultaneously sending it off to its place in cinema history.

Brosnan had to break free of his James Bond persona to capture the kind of Americanized bravado McTiernan wanted in his Thomas Crown, but he had to do so in minute ways of mannerism and attitude. In the early days of the shoot, Brosnan was still carrying that James Bond urgency in his shoulders when he walked. It didn't quite fit in with the carefree playboy attitude of Crown. McTiernan and Brosnan worked on the stride until it became a confident Stateside strut, much looser but confident in a different way than Bond. James Bond carried concern in his movements; Crown had not a care in the world.

The Irish-born Brosnan had never golfed, either, so he took a few weeks of lessons to learn how to swing the club. His Crown character never makes contact with the ball on screen, but he had to at least *look* like he knew what he was doing with the club in his hand.

Where he was a bank robber in the original film, in McTiernan's version Thomas Crown would be an art thief. The robbery in the original film is an armed robbery, and a bank thief carries with it more violent, menacing connotations simply because of the nature of the heist; a wealthy executive nabbing famous works of art is decidedly less threatening to general audiences, and it set the breezy tone. (It was the exact opposite alteration he made in the *Die Hard: With a Vengeance* storyline, where Simon and his band of criminals were originally art thieves until they became pillagers of gold bullion.)

22. Silver Lining

Before filming began, the biggest aesthetic decision McTiernan made was to employ an outdated technology for a big chunk of the movie: the dolly track. Before Steadicam technology became the industry standard for so many films, dolly tracks were the most common ways to capture fluid movement. The technique involved building complex railing systems along the floor of sets, using the rails to move the camera in and out during scenes, and interchanging long and short lenses for reach and focus depending on what the scene required. The Steadicam, which can be used to zoom in and out and does not require the same cumbersome rail system, all but replaced dolly tracking by the late 1990s. McTiernan saw the merit in using a classic technique for a lighthearted caper film, giving it a retro feel; the dolly shots would paint the story with an old-school fluidity, and a sense of ballet movement at certain moments as the story and the adventure unfolded.[1]

The dolly tracking system was so outdated by the late '90s that McTiernan had a tough time finding a dolly grip to operate the equipment. He and his cinematographer, Tom Priestly, wound up training William Jones—a camera team member who had a little experience in the past with dolly usage—to operate it.

The extended opening museum sequence that would set up the rest of the film was to take place inside the New York Metropolitan Museum on Central Park East. But those in charge of the museum were not keen on being the victim of a theft, however outlandish the caper would turn out to be in the movie. This forced McTiernan to use a Fifth Avenue library for the interior entryway of the museum; the buildings had two distinct, dissimilar grand entrances, but those in the audience keen enough to pick up on the difference would be minimal in the grand scheme of things. Art exhibits would be built on sets either way due to the moving parts required—and the various types of damage that would occur—to film the elaborate heist. The Metropolitan had no say regarding the exterior of the building, however, so McTiernan was able to grab establishing exterior shots of the museum to intercut with the library and the sets.[2]

McTiernan had another minor issue to work around. To steal the painting, Crown would have to rip the Monet out of its frame and fold it in a briefcase he had stashed beneath a bench. The art department worked with McTiernan to figure out an elaborate contraption for the briefcase that would carefully break the frame so it could be logically folded. But focus groups that saw early versions of the film were still a bit troubled that such a famous work of art would be mutilated and mashed together inside a case.

To get around this, McTiernan simply trimmed the scene. Rather than trying to think of some new way for Crown to sneak the painting into the briefcase, therein creating more re-shoots, he simply kept the action of the folding to a minimum. He cut from the moment the frame is broken, to a medium shot of Brosnan; the briefcase is closed and latched almost entirely offscreen. And later, when Crown is putting the painting in his study, little attention is placed on the briefcase opening and the painting coming out. It was a simple trick, and a subtle manipulation of the viewer's attention, focusing instead on Brosnan's performance.

The climax of this opening scene where Crown makes off with the painting is shot primarily using the dolly tracking system. It gives the action a palpable sense of continuous motion and energy that would be hard to execute with any other technique. Conversations between Russo's Banning and Leary's Michael in the backlit museum, in the aftermath of the heist, used the dolly system to ebb and flow with whomever was speaking at the time.

McTiernan also had another opportunity here to play with subtitles. In *The Hunt for Red October* and *The 13th Warrior*, McTiernan chose specific moments of conversation to subtly shift the language from subtitles to English for the remainder of the film. It allowed the audience to focus on the performances and the action rather than reading the words on the bottom of the screen. This time, McTiernan didn't bother with subtitles at all.

In an early interrogation scene between Russo's Catherine Banning and one of the bumbling patsy thieves from the museum robbery, Banning is speaking in the thief's native Romanian. McTiernan went with subtitles in the beginning, but he decided rather quickly that they were taking away the real intention of the scene; this was all about Russo as Banning, slinking towards this timid robber, almost wrapping her body around him like a serpent seducing its prey. It was one of the earliest moments where McTiernan wanted to show off Banning's sexual prowess, rendering dialogue useless.

The second act of the film would develop the steamy sexual relationship between Crown and Banning, and most of it would take place on Crown's island hideaway on the French Caribbean island of Martinique. This was McTiernan's first real venture into extensive sex scenes, and he

22. Silver Lining

opted to use the dolly technology here as well. The dolly shots as Crown and Banning begin their affair in his New York apartment were kept at a distance for two specific purposes: to enhance the intimacy of the moment, and to give the act itself a dreamlike quality, the lovers seemingly suspended in midair throes of passion. Shots were fleeting and distant, but the two subjects would be lit against a darkened background, so the audience could focus less on the act and more on the passion between the two characters.

McTiernan also switched out the polo game scene from the original with a boat race, but he did keep the glider scene. They had stuntmen do the in-air gymnastics inside the glider, and for the close-ups he had Brosnan and McTiernan in the glider on the ground—the aerial scenery would be added in postproduction. Only McTiernan could not fit a camera in the cabin of the glider with both actors, so he installed a mirror right in front of Russo and shot the reflection in the mirror from the exterior.

In an ironic twist of fate, *The Thomas Crown Affair* was released August 6, 1999, just three weeks before *The 13th Warrior*. Critics were mostly kind to the finished product, admiring the fun performances from its two leads, and adult audiences sought it out. It opened fourth with a respectable $20 million box-office haul, and finished its theatrical run just

Rene Russo and Pierce Brosnan in *The Thomas Crown Affair* (MGM Studios, 1999).

shy of $70 million against a budget of $48 million.³ A success. And it also surpassed the entire international haul of *The 13th Warrior*, which came in $100 million shy of its own price tag. It was quite an interesting dichotomy of success and failure in a single month's time for McTiernan, though it was clear of which film he was most proud.

McTiernan would spend the next several months working on court cases, and trying to get his personal life in some order before getting back behind the camera. His next film, another remake, took him right back into the Norman Jewison filmography.

It may have sounded like the right idea at the time.

23

The Catherine Banning Affair

Pierce Brosnan's slick businessman and part-time art thief might be the title character of *The Thomas Crown Affair*, but something is made perfectly clear as the story advances: this is a film about the journey of Rene Russo's Catherine Banning.

John McTiernan paid special attention to the Banning character that is, by the sheer fact that forty-five-year-old Russo is cast in the role, the most important character in the film. Movies like *The Thomas Crown Affair*, blithe adult capers with intense romances at their core, had almost exclusively involved an older actor and a romantic lead who is five, or ten, or maybe fifteen years younger than the male protagonist. The original Thomas Crown is a perfect example, with a thirty-eight-year-old Steve McQueen romancing twenty-seven-year-old Faye Dunaway. The same year as McTiernan's remake, the teacher/student heist film *Entrapment* featured a sixty-nine-year-old Sean Connery in a battle of wits against a twenty-nine-year-old Catherine Zeta-Jones.

The age disparity between actor and actress subconsciously allows the male lead to play the dominant force in the relationship. Even when romance is not directly involved, as with the aforementioned *Entrapment*, the fact that the male lead is the older of the two implies his being the wiser. Not this time around, however.

The early scene where Banning is interrogating one of the pitiful criminals, where McTiernan opted to remove unimportant subtitles from the scene, is one of the first instances where McTiernan worked to build Banning's sexual independence. Instead of reading, the viewer grows captivated by Russo's performance, as Banning pushes in on this weaker male thief, manipulating him with her overt sexuality. She squeezes a confession from the thief, who finds himself almost powerless in her presence.

From early in the film Catherine Banning is set up not as an object of desire for Thomas Crown, but a romantic equal. She is less enthralled with Crown than she sees him as a worthy adversary in her own game. There is a moment after one of their first dates together where Crown, working on an assumption, makes a move to insinuate he will be following Banning upstairs to her apartment. With a telling glance and playful glare, Banning pushes back his advances, taking immediate control of the situation. This character is in charge of her body more than most female leads in Hollywood movies, including Faye Dunaway's Vicki in the original *Thomas Crown Affair*, who is left in bed by McQueen's Crown, wilting like a dry flower. Banning, on the other hand, will let Crown know when *she* is ready to take their relationship to the next level.

Crown and Banning are both hardened characters who commit wholly to their work and leave romantic relationships sidelined; that is, until they met each other. It is likely that neither of them had ever maintained a long-term relationship. Keeping their love lives in check is a form of control, and that is not a trait exclusively belonging to Crown.

Once these two rulers of their respective realms fall into each other's arms, following a sexually charged dance sequence, McTiernan stages many of these passionate moments with an acute attention to Banning's orientation in the shot. An early glimpse of the two naked and making their way across Crown's apartment frames Russo in Brosnan's arms, but lifted above his head and looking down. While it represents Crown's strength, it is an intentionally dominant blocking setup for Banning as she towers over her prey.

There is a scene shortly thereafter where the two lovers lie together, naked in bed, and this is a clear indicator that McTiernan wants to replace Dunaway's weakened character with the confident, imposing persona of Catherine Banning. Rather than have Banning lie next to Crown in bed, framed in the background behind him, McTiernan shoots the scene with Banning draped over the top of him. The shot is a strong visual cue regarding the relationship dynamics of these two characters. Banning is in charge.

The sex scenes in the picture are tastefully framed and steeped in eroticism more so than physicality or shock value; and they are some of the most electric, scorching scenes of their kind, at least in a lighthearted caper movie of this ilk. The scenes were out of McTiernan's comfort zone as a filmmaker—eroticism in the 1990s belonged to directors like Adrian

23. The Catherine Banning Affair

Lyne—but he has always been eager to tell a new romance in a familiar setting.[1] What he helps create, in turn, is the pinnacle performance in Rene Russo's career.

Banning is not only a sexually liberated female lead, and the perfect romantic foil for Thomas Crown, she is confident in all avenues of her life. She is perfectly unkempt in her mannerisms, gulping a can of soda right out of the vending machine or choking down green goop while she paces the police station break room; her hair is never entirely in place, but she is always dressed impeccably and brimming with confidence, parading her feminine power and flaunting her independence in the presence of these flummoxed New York cops. When she eventually does sleep with Crown, Banning is not simply swept up by some charming scoundrel; she knows the angles too, and she plays the game right along with him.

The relationship between Banning and Denis Leary's sad-sack detective, Michael McCann, is another interesting power play working in Banning's advantage. McCann clearly fancies her, but he is almost immediately

Pierce Brosnan and Rene Russo take a break in the glider on the set of *The Thomas Crown Affair* (MGM Studios, 1999).

intimidated by her Alpha female confidence. She wears incredible, expensive clothing, she floats through life with seemingly nothing to weigh her down, and even though she shares this theft investigation with McCann, she could not be from a place less accessible to him.

It could be argued that Banning is ultimately punished for her sexual individuality. She falls in love with Crown, and shortly thereafter she is shown photos (given to her by McCann, who of course wants Catherine to himself) of Crown with a mysterious young blonde. Their relationship fractures, and Banning has moments where her confidence has clearly been broken. She cries on the stairs, she stands in the rain, set adrift by the emotional attachment she felt with Crown, pushed away from her stern presence into just another victim of love.

McTiernan and costume designers Kate Harrington and Mark Zunino intentionally soften Banning's attire as she begins to gradually open herself up to Crown. This is not a punishment, but a breach of the emotional wall she had built around herself. It breaks her down, sure, and we have moments watching her trying to get that hardened persona back in place. It doesn't work. She has finally found an emotional attachment, and she is not so much punished for this as knocked off her center. Banning has changed, and in these moments her arc becomes the focus of the entire film.

Thomas Crown is the title character, but he exists in the background of his own story, creating various catalysts in order for the plot to move forward. His emotional journey takes a definite backseat to the evolution of Catherine Banning, however. Make no mistake, Rene Russo is the lead character from just about every conceivable angle, no matter what the title says.

Part VII

Downward Spiral

24

Rollerball

The court battle involving John McTiernan, Donna Dubrow, and their Wyoming neighbors, Sam and Mona Scott, which had begun over abandoned water rights and usage, was still stumbling through the state's legal system in the fall of 1999, two years after the suit had been filed. Semantic arguments regarding how much acreage was being irrigated or not and how much had been *truly* abandoned by the Scotts kept the case busy in appeals court hearings.[1] It was just a distraction for McTiernan, whose domestic situation with Donna Dubrow had only gotten worse. While the two of them pushed back against the Scotts, their own divorce hearing was growing more contentious by the day. McTiernan's trust in Dubrow was weakening, just as his mistrust in Hollywood was intensifying.

To complicate matters further, in June of 2000 McTiernan became a father when his girlfriend Kate Harrington gave birth to their daughter, Truman Elizabeth McTiernan. His personal life was going in a dozen different directions at once, and he needed another film project in which to dive headfirst to help take his mind off his troubles.

But, in retrospect, it may not have been the best time to direct again.

Seven years and three films after Norman Jewison directed *The Thomas Crown Affair*, he dove into the world of a futuristic blood sport set in a dystopian society, where corporations have become the governing body of the people. The film, from writer William Harrison, was called *Rollerball*, and it was a modest hit for MGM in the summer of 1975. Over the years, it's become a minor cult classic, but it was absolutely a picture defined by the decade in which it was released. It is still a clever, well-designed thriller, but *Rollerball* was ripe for a remake since the last twenty-five years brought with it opportunities for technological advancement and an entirely different world outlook. Not only had the geopolitical climate

Part VII: Downward Spiral

changed drastically from 1975 to the new millennium, the map of the world itself had quite literally changed several times.

McTiernan saw, once again, a chance to try something new in his career. He signed on to direct, and he also decided to produce the film alongside a pair of producers: Beau St. Clair and a rising star in Hollywood named Charles Roven. The time felt right, and the first screenplay for this remake may have even transcended Jewison's original, at least in the eyes of the few who saw it.

Little-known screenwriter David Campbell Wilson submitted the first draft for a new *Rollerball*. Just about everyone who managed to read Wilson's screenplay was impressed by his work. His story, which took place roughly four hundred years in the future, opened up the fictional mechanics of the sport, adding layers of strategy and details to the gameplay in order to heighten realism and create a more involving product from which the story could develop. What's more, Wilson's *Rollerball* was a heady look at a futuristic dystopian society, and his story would focus on the materialistic nature of modern culture and explore what sort of totalitarian regime might lead us down this path. Wilson had people excited that this new film would be better than the original. One person, however, did not much care for the direction Wilson went with the story: the director.[2]

John McTiernan had his own express vision for this new *Rollerball*, one that was not as concerned with corrupted social mores and subtle themes about government oppression as it was with showcasing action and violence in a kinetic, fluid action spectacle. He wanted his story to focus on the game itself far more than the world outside the arena, focusing the bulk of his energy on the violent blood sport and capturing an aesthetic that would please the MTV crowd. He therefore commissioned John Pogue to write a screenplay in the vein of his specific, albeit confusing, vision.

With an assist from *The Hunt for Red October* scribe Larry Ferguson, Pogue returned with a screenplay that focused primarily on the sporting action, and a greedy Russian villain looking to improve his ratings through fabricated violence in the games. It was an odd bit of irony, bringing in Ferguson; his *Hunt for Red October* screenplay wanted to eschew the technical exposition of Clancy's novel for a more action-centric picture, and McTiernan rejected the idea in 1989. Now, here he was, tasking Ferguson with ramping up the action for *Rollerball* while trimming away the intellectual tapestry.

The time period was inexplicably changed from the twenty-fifth century to 2005, just a few years down the road. Maybe the idea was to make the audience think that we, as a society, were not that far from this dystopian world as a whole; or perhaps it was a budgetary decision. Setting a film five years down the road required much less set design and innovation than a film taking place in the distant future. Whatever the case for the peculiar time change in the plot, McTiernan felt Pogue and Ferguson's new screenplay was more in line with the story he wanted to tell.

For some reason, the music-video crowd seduced McTiernan in the late 1990s. Music videos were still crucial cultural works of often frenetic art when the calendar changed to the new millennium, and McTiernan wanted to direct what amounted to an extended music-video/ESPN highlight package movie. This explained the decision to redo the original screenplay. Also, rather than employing a few hundred cuts in the editing room, as was standard with his previous action films, McTiernan wanted thousands of cuts. He wanted the visual side of the story to be constantly on the move, certain this would create a breathless action film that would be able to tap into the youth in the country and make the movie a success.

On one hand, catering to this demographic made pragmatic sense; Hollywood is a business first and foremost, and the primary goal is to make money. Nobody occupies movie theaters more than teenagers, so getting them on board with a high-flying, frenetic action spectacle was key; if the teenage crowd was excited that meant ticket sales. It sounded like a foolproof plan in McTiernan's mind, even if his producer, Charles Roven, seemed less than convinced.

The screenplay was settled and McTiernan had his *Rollerball* vision firmly locked in place; rarely did he storyboard his movies ahead of time, and save for the biggest action sequences this story was planted only in his imagination.

Now came the work of casting the right people. At one point during pre-production, McTiernan was certain Keanu Reeves was coming on board as Jonathan Cross, the leader of the team and the hero of the story.[3] But the years following the success of *The Matrix* were busy ones for Reeves, who was in the middle of a six-films-in-three-years stretch. After *The Matrix* in 1999, Reeves starred in the football comedy *The Replacements*; the serial-killer potboiler *The Watcher*; *The Gift*, wherein he played an abusive husband; the terminal-illness romance *Sweet November*; and a baseball-themed family film, *Hardball*—all before *Rollerball* even hit theaters.

It could have been Reeves's tricky schedule that steered him away from the project, but it also could have been Charles Roven who thought a young, fresh face in the lead role would make more sense.

Chris Klein had only been in five feature films before he was hired to play Jonathan Cross, the rookie superstar on the Horsemen, the main team in *Rollerball*. It may sound like a healthy enough number of films for Klein to be given the keys to drive McTiernan's action film, but those five features included two supporting parts in the teen ensemble *American Pie* films, a completely forgotten raunchy comedy called *Say It Isn't So*, and an equally overlooked romance called *Here on Earth*. Klein's debut film was a small role in Alexander Payne's seminal high-school politics satire, *Election*, but his role as a dumb jock was played for laughs. Klein only had two opportunities to headline his own movie with *Say It Isn't So* and *Here on Earth*, and neither of them had been even moderately successful. He resembled Reeves physically, with his dark hair and fair skin, but he had a passivity to his voice that did not fit in with such a hardened dystopia. Yet, here he was, cast as the lead in a futuristic action movie that was aiming for a Memorial Day 2001 release. This was an entirely different ballgame, and Klein did not seem primed for the spotlight. The plan was to have *Rollerball* be Klein's breakout hero role, one that would catapult him to superstardom. McTiernan eventually bought into the casting because Klein had an all-American look and a wholesome demeanor that would provide a terrific juxtaposition to the brutality of the film.

LL Cool J was cast to play team captain Marcus Ridley. The former hip-hop artist had turned his attention to acting in the late 1980s with a bit role in the football comedy *Wildcats*. In 1991, he grabbed a supporting role in the action-comedy *The Hard Way*, and the following year he did the same in Barry Levinson's high-concept disaster, *Toys*. It was an inauspicious beginning for LL Cool J the actor, but none of these early films failed because of his direct involvement. In fact, he was a strong enough screen presence that acting soon became his primary job over music. By 2001 he had starred in a handful of films, including *Halloween: H2O*, and Oliver Stone's clumsy football opus, *Any Given Sunday*.

Perhaps McTiernan was mentally referring back to the casting decisions he made on *Predator*, when he brought in Carl Weathers to act alongside Arnold Schwarzenegger in order to get the best performance possible from the Austrian superstar. LL Cool J was an actor with a substantial bit more experience than Klein, and maybe he could push Klein to be the leading man everyone involved with *Rollerball* hoped he would be.

Next up was finding the female lead, a tough Eastern European teammate of Jonathan and Marcus named Aurora, who also becomes Jonathan's lover very early on in the film. Too early on to be believable, actually. For Aurora, casting director Pat McCorkle brought in a burgeoning Southern California model turned actress named Rebecca Romijn-Stamos.

After getting her start as a model for *Sports Illustrated*, Victoria's Secret, and Christian Dior, Rebecca Romijn-Stamos began transitioning to acting in the late 1990s. She appeared in one episode of *Friends*, and nabbed cameos in *Austin Powers: The Spy Who Shagged Me* and the Norm MacDonald comedy *Dirty Work* before getting a recurring role on the sitcom *Just Shoot Me!* Her big break came, ironically, as an unrecognizable blue mutant in Bryan Singer's 2000 superhero film *X-Men*. She played the shape-shifting villainess Mystique, and even though she had almost no lines and very little to do in the film beyond physical feats, her unique appearance—the scaly blue skin and orange hair stood out in Singer's otherwise steely-gray film—was enough to kick-start her career as a film actress.

Rebecca Romijn-Stamos and John McTiernan discuss a shot on the set of *Rollerball* (MGM Pictures, 2002).

Part VII: Downward Spiral

McTiernan saw a blank slate with Romijn-Stamos, a California blonde who needed to darken her appearance and harden her exterior to play the scarred, exploited Russian athlete. He put her in a black wig, caked on the eyeliner and dark mascara, and ran a scar from above her right eye down to her right cheek. The costuming for Romijn-Stamos (put in place by McTiernan's girlfriend at the time, costume designer Kate Harrington) would allow her to open up as a character that is so drastically different from the California model's true personality. At least that was McTiernan's vision.

To play the villain, Russian rollerball promoter and ratings hound Alexis Petrovich, McTiernan brought in Jean Reno, the go-to actor specializing in the European villain types. Despite the fact that the Moroccan-born Reno had broken out in America playing Léon, the hitman with a heart of gold, in Luc Besson's *The Professional*, Reno had steadily gravitated to playing the villain in big-budget action films like *Mission: Impossible*, *Ronin*, and the 1998 remake of *Godzilla*. Reno was no star, not by any means, and by the time the '90s came to a close his bankability had dissipated considerably. He was not going to move the needle one way or another as the villain, but he was a competent actor and he could snarl with the best of them.

With the cast in place, John McTiernan and his team headed to the Northeast, across the border to Blainville, Québec, a suburban area just north of Montreal. Filming began in July of 2000, and almost immediately things went south.

Charles Roven had been working consistently in Hollywood as a producer since the early 1980s. His first project as producer was, to bring things full circle, *Heart Like a Wheel*, the Bonnie Bedelia film that Bruce Willis referenced when he mentioned hiring her for *Die Hard*. From there, Roven shuffled along, producing B-pictures like the *Mad Max* rip-off *The Blood of Heroes*, a moderately successful Robin Williams dark comedy called *Cadillac Man*, and the psycho-sexual thriller *Final Analysis* starring Richard Gere and Kim Basinger. In 1995, Roven finally produced a legitimate hit movie, Terry Gilliam's *Twelve Monkeys*. The grungy science-fiction thriller was critically praised and almost doubled its budget at the box office.

The success of *Twelve Monkeys* served as a launch pad for Roven, who followed it up with the Denzel Washington thriller *Fallen*, the Nicolas Cage/Meg Ryan romantic drama *City of Angels*—which turned into a massive

24. Rollerball

hit—and the David O. Russell Gulf War drama *Three Kings*. The string of hits sent Roven's career into a new stratosphere of power and influence in Hollywood, and made him one of the hottest producers in the industry when he came on board *Rollerball*.

Roven and John McTiernan were not in sync as to what sort of movie *Rollerball* should be, and their two egos allegedly collided all throughout production. The source of the friction could have been screenplay disputes, or it could have been something as simple as two Alpha males trying to control their environment. Accounts of the rift vary depending on who is telling the story. Whatever the case, rumors abounded that McTiernan was growing increasingly paranoid that Roven and the production company were undermining his work on the film to make sure it was a failure. It was the same suspicion McTiernan felt when Shane Black and David Arnott stepped into Arnold Schwarzenegger's trailer on the set of *Last Action Hero*.

Then, only a month into the shoot, there was the fire. It did not help things.

On August 3, a small fire broke out in the locker-room set, which was inside a Blainville warehouse. Carpenters working on the set tried to extinguish the flames but were unsuccessful. Firefighters arrived and put everything out, but not before a great deal of the locker room and its props and camera equipment were damaged and in need of replacement.[4] The fire, reported as an electrical malfunction, caused a substantial delay in the middle of the shoot and only spurred McTiernan's increasing paranoia.[5]

He then allegedly made a decision that would haunt him for the rest of his life.

The Montreal production of *Rollerball* wrapped in November of 2000, but McTiernan had to travel to San Francisco with Chris Klein and LL Cool J to film the opening body-board racing sequence. He wrapped the complicated opening race in April 2001, and immediately submitted an epic, R-rated version of the film, which ran well over two hours. The initial test audience reactions were almost wholly negative, so much so that the release date was moved from Memorial Day weekend in 2001 to mid–July. The studio wanted to put together a new series of test screenings in hopes that the audience was out there for McTiernan's movie. They just needed to find them.

McTiernan had his own idea for a private screening.

The Internet was only about a decade old in 2001, at least when it

Part VII: Downward Spiral

came to societal availability. Newspaper and magazine critics were still the deciding factor when it came to a film's success or failure, but that was rapidly changing in the earliest days of the twenty-first century. Information online began moving at speeds too brisk for much of the print media to keep up. Opinions were being voiced for everyone to see, all around the world, and a handful of film fanatics and pop-culture geeks were in the forefront of the Internet film-critic explosion. Film discussion and analysis was migrating, along with everything else, to the Web.

One of the pioneers of online film news and criticism was an Austin, Texas, native named Harry Knowles, who began molding his online identity as early as 1994 when he was a twenty-three-year-old movie buff. He would cobble together news and rumors on upcoming films, and eventually turned his Internet presence into one of the first film news and reviews websites, Ain't It Cool News. The site was a success almost immediately, and Knowles began getting invites into the world of the mainstream media. Knowles, an excitable and eccentric movie nut with a shock of red hair and a beard to match, had turned his unabashed fandom into one of the first voices of a new generation of kids who sought opinions and updates online rather than in print.[6]

The news of the *Rollerball* remake was one of Knowles's crusades in the late 1990s. Knowles was a huge fan of the 1975 original, and he tracked the ups and downs of McTiernan's remake from the first news reports. He was not a fan of the news he was hearing. From the casting decisions to the questionable screenplay alterations—Knowles had read David Campbell Wilson's original screenplay and, like most people who had done so, he thought it was brilliant—he heavily criticized the film's production on multiple occasions. The swipes he was taking at the film caught the attention of McTiernan, who saw an opportunity to maybe change Knowles's mind in one of the more bizarre and unprecedented publicity stunts in film history.

On June 4, 2001, about a month after initial test audiences resoundingly rejected McTiernan's first cut of *Rollerball*, the director called Harry Knowles personally and invited him to a screening of the film in Long Island, New York. Knowles, his father, and a fellow writer for Ain't It Cool News named Quint, met McTiernan at an Austin airfield at one in the morning. The flight took off at two, and the next morning Knowles saw a cut of the film with McTiernan and a handful of MGM executives in attendance.

24. Rollerball

The plan all along was for Knowles to report on the screening on his website. It was a good idea in theory, and however strange it was it fit in with McTiernan's plan all along, to have his movie appeal to a younger teenage audience like the ones who were perusing Ain't It Cool News on a daily basis. To Knowles's credit, however, he did not feel any pressure to praise the film.

While Knowles admired the brutality, his criticisms were aimed at things that were beyond repair. His biggest issue was with Chris Klein, who lacked charisma. Klein's performance, Knowles pointed out, was disastrous. He also took issue with the game at the center of the film, which had no real structure or officials or scoreboard, and the gameplay action was an indecipherable mess.

Knowles's report on the print sent the studio into full-blown panic mode; it was a feeling all too familiar for McTiernan, whose *13th Warrior* disaster was still in his rearview mirror. MGM began to order massive re-shoots and sweeping edits to tone down the violence for a PG-13 crowd, even though that had been the one area Harry Knowles praised. But this was about selling tickets now, about salvaging the film's bottom line at the box office, regardless of the quality. Nudity and bloodshed were trimmed away first, and the release date was moved from July 2001 to February 2002, where it could be hidden. McTiernan was not happy; even though his vision of the film was probably the wrong one, he was upset at more studio meddling. The damage had been done, and the studio was trying to fix their $70 million potential disaster in any way they could.

No matter what sort of spin control they tried in the editing room and with re-shoots, *Rollerball* was already infamous, due in no small part to Knowles's critique. It was another "troubled production," the third major malfunction of its kind in McTiernan's career, and now the information could get out there more quickly and in more detail. When *Rollerball* finally hit theaters on February 8, 2002, it was, predictably, lambasted by critics and met with an astounding wave of audience indifference.

Rollerball opened third that weekend with nearly $11 million, but word of mouth traveled at lightning speed in the new age of Internet critics, the very medium McTiernan had tried to embrace. Despite a month in the theaters, *Rollerball* wound up with a flaccid $19 million domestic haul. The $6 million foreign gross only added insult to injury. It was a failure by any metric.[7]

In a half-hearted attempt to repair *Rollerball*'s image and hopefully recoup some of the lost box-office numbers, MGM released the R-rated version of the film for the Special Edition DVD. It was the only edition to hit home video. The R-rated version added roughly three minutes of footage, including a few topless shots of Rebecca Romijn-Stamos. It was not enough, and very few people cared enough to buy the DVD and see more violence and nudity.

25

Dodging a Bullet

In the summer of 2001, right around the same time John McTiernan was calling up Harry Knowles and inviting him to Long Island to screen *Rollerball*, he was already mapping out his next project: *Basic Instinct 2*.

The original *Basic Instinct* was a lurid sexual thriller that made a superstar out of Sharon Stone; it also brought with it more than a little controversy. Gay and lesbian organizations in and around San Francisco, the story's setting, protested the film for its depiction of the homosexual lifestyle. In the face of whatever protestations or controversies (or perhaps *because* of this extra publicity), Paul Verhoeven's hyper-violent potboiler pulled in over $117 million in 1993, the ninth-best haul for the year.[1]

Following the success of the original, *Basic Instinct 2* was bound to happen. Until it wasn't. Carolco Pictures funded the original and owned the rights to any sequels, but by 1997 the company had buckled under the failures of *Last of the Dogmen*, *Showgirls*, and the calamitous pirate adventure *Cutthroat Island*.[2] MGM swooped in and bought the rights to *Basic Instinct* with the plan to create a series of films in the vein of the original, but without Sharon Stone's involvement. It would be an anthology featuring a different femme fatale each time, all under the umbrella of the *Basic Instinct* name.

Then, three years later, in a miraculous reversal of fortune, Carolco re-emerged as C2 thanks to the collaborative efforts of Carolco's owner, Mario Kassar, and producer Andrew G. Vajna. They immediately re-acquired the rights to *Basic Instinct* from MGM, who had not been able to get any of those franchise films off the ground. They offered Stone a $13 million salary to return. She agreed, and the project was green lit with a screenplay from Leora Barish and Henry Bean. *Basic Instinct 2: Risk Addiction* was its full title, and it needed a director.

Canadian horror *auteur* David Cronenberg was offered the job, but he passed. Action filmmaker Lee Tamahori declined the project as well before it found its way into John McTiernan's hands. McTiernan agreed to do the sequel; but, much like with *Rollerball*, he wanted to rebuild the screenplay from the ground up.

In the Barish and Bean script, Stone's Catherine Tramell seduces a psychiatrist hired to evaluate her after she is implicated in another murder. McTiernan wanted to keep the psychiatrist angle intact, but he wanted to change the social status of the male protagonist. Rather than have him as a traditional therapist with an office and a couch, McTiernan envisioned him as a resident psychiatrist working long hours for half the pay in a city hospital. Not only would he be seduced by Tramell, he would also be drawn into her web of wealth and opulence.

McTiernan also wanted to lower the age of the male lead, making him a bit younger than Stone as opposed to her peer, even though he had ignored such a discrepancy in *The Thomas Crown Affair*. He specifically wanted Benjamin Bratt for the role. Although Bratt was only five years younger than Stone, he had a youthfulness, vitality, and a baby face that could make him appear much younger. McTiernan saw star potential in Bratt, but Stone had final say on the male lead. She rejected Bratt. McTiernan, perhaps sensing another troubled production looming, decided to abandon the project once Bratt was rejected.

McTiernan's exodus stopped *Basic Instinct 2* dead in its tracks. Vajna and Kassar moved on to a third *Terminator* film, but Stone almost immediately filed a lawsuit against them for violation of an oral agreement. The case remained open for three years before Vajna and Kassar agreed to pay Stone; rather than pay her off, however, the producers green lit the sequel once again and paid Stone to reprise her role, hoping to at least get some income from the headache. Journeyman director Michael Caton-Jones was brought into the fold, and relative unknown David Morrissey was cast as the male lead. The sequel became more of an obligation than any sort of attempt to craft a clever follow-up to the original.

Basic Instinct 2 was an unmitigated disaster, quickly becoming a punch line and foundering at the box office. McTiernan dodged a bullet, because another complete failure would have almost certainly ended his career in Hollywood. What he did not realize at the time was that he might have already ended his career on his own.

26

Basic

McTiernan was clearly eager to move on to a new project before he even finished butchering *Rollerball* at the behest of MGM and the producers. *Basic Instinct 2* was that new project for a while, but he jumped ship once it was apparent his vision for the film was not going to happen. Instead, he went for a labyrinthine military thriller from a young screenwriter named James Vanderbilt.

Basic fancied itself a military version of *Rashomon*, Akira Kurosawa's 1950 mystery thriller where the same crime is recounted from different points of view. Vanderbilt's screenplay told the story of a celebrated army ranger, who disappears during a routine training mission, and the DEA agent hired to investigate said disappearance. His investigation, with the help of a local military police officer, would take place through varying first-hand accounts of a murder in the jungle. John Travolta was already cast as the DEA agent, Tom Hardy, before McTiernan came on board.

By the early 2000s, John Travolta had experienced the highs and lows of stardom in Hollywood more than once. A breakout young star in the late 1970s with the back-to-back dance hits *Saturday Night Fever* and *Grease*, the New Jersey native quickly turned this early success into a flourishing acting career. From those two hit films, Travolta headlined a Texas workingman drama named *Urban Cowboy* and Brian DePalma's conspiracy thriller *Blow Out*.

He scuffled through most of the 1980s in forgettable features before finding some moderate success in the 1989 family comedy *Look Who's Talking*, which was subsequently run into the ground with a pair of dreadful sequels. And then, 1994 happened.

A young filmmaker named Quentin Tarantino took a chance casting John Travolta in his new crime-drama, *Pulp Fiction*, playing a heroin-

Part VII: Downward Spiral

addicted hit man who serves as the fractured, time-jumping narrative's through-line. The film would change cinema forever, and it would put Travolta back on top again. He was nominated for an Academy Award for Best Actor, only the second of his career and the first one since *Saturday Night Fever* back in 1977.[1]

It was not simply the success of *Pulp Fiction* that changed Travolta's fortune as an actor; it was the type of role. Vincent Vega was a scoundrel and a drug addict and a killer, something Travolta had never even come close to playing in his career. It showed off a different side of him as an actor, and in the afterglow of *Pulp Fiction* he tried his hand at a wide range of films.

He played opposite Harry Belafonte in the race-reversal drama *White Man's Burden*; he played loan shark and aspiring filmmaker Chili Palmer in the hugely successful adaptation of Elmore Leonard's *Get Shorty*. He played a slovenly angel in *Michael*, an everyman with sudden powers in *Phenomenon*, and he teamed up with Asian action director John Woo for a pair of blockbusters, the second of which was the incredible snapshot of the '90s action zeitgeist, *Face/Off*. It was an incredible run of success for Travolta.

And then, just like it did in the 1980s, his career hit the skids. But this was the twenty-first century so his demise was much more public, especially when his passion project, *Battlefield Earth*, became one of the biggest commercial and critical disasters of all time. It became the new shorthand answer for awful movies, all but tarnishing the goodwill Travolta had built up over the last six years. He followed *Battlefield Earth* with another high-profile failure in *Swordfish*, a film that became more famous for the gratuitous topless shot of Halle Berry than anything the movie had to offer in the way of compelling plot or performances.[2]

By 2001, Travolta was squarely in the middle of another ebb in his career, and perhaps he saw another chance to step outside his comfort zone as an actor with *Basic* and possibly reinvent himself for a third time. Whatever drew him to the project, he and McTiernan quickly developed a strong working relationship.

As for the tyrannical Sergeant West, McTiernan and his team were dead-set on bringing in Samuel L. Jackson. McTiernan and Jackson worked beautifully together during *Die Hard: With a Vengeance*. In the years since, Jackson's star had only risen. Always the busy actor, he had starred in massive hits like *A Time to Kill* and *Unbreakable*, a second film with Tarantino in *Jackie Brown*, and a glut of hits and misses jam-packed into six years.

26. Basic

John McTiernan (left) and John Travolta discussing a scene on the set of *Basic* (Columbia Pictures, 2003).

The West character begged for a fiery performer like Jackson, who rarely declined a role anyway.

Jackson and John Travolta would be reunited on *Basic*, but where they spent the majority of their screen time together in *Pulp Fiction* they would share only a few brief moments this time around. Jackson's appearances would be spent with an impressive collection of young talent like Taye Diggs, Giovanni Ribisi, and Brian Van Holt. Meanwhile, Travolta would share most of his scenes with Connie Nielsen, who played the plucky military detective Osborne.

The Danish-born Nielsen with her open, vulnerable face and lean physique had shown versatility, slipping in between period pieces and modern stories with incredible ease. Prior to *Basic*, for example, Nielsen starred in Ridley Scott's *Gladiator* and the micro-budget Robin Williams indie thriller *One Hour Photo* back to back. They were two films that were antithetical to each other, but two films that benefited from Nielsen's presence. It was that combination of versatility and edge, her ability to attack roles with a no-nonsense approach that McTiernan loved, because he knew the success of *Basic* would hinge on the mismatched energies of the eccentric Travolta and the straight-edged Nielsen.

Ahead of the shoot, Nielsen spent time on military bases with female officers, copping their attitudes and posture and digging into what they used to stand their ground in a male-centric military world. When she arrived for the first day of filming, Monday the 26th of November, 2001, Nielsen brought with her a fully realized character, from the top of her cropped hair down to the soles of her G. I. boots.

The shoot took place in the jungles of Panama and a military base in Jacksonville, Florida, save for a few minor secondary shots and sets. What drew McTiernan to the story from the start was one moment in Vanderbilt's screenplay: Hardy and Osborne play a good cop/bad cop routine on a witness and Hardy sabotages the situation. It was the template for the mood of the entire picture, and McTiernan leaned into breezy double-cross nature by allowing his camera to whip and roll and move without the same discipline he had brought to his earlier work.[3]

Most screenplays average roughly one page of dialogue per one minute of screen time, but many sections of *Basic* squeezed in around two pages of dialogue per minute. To combat this, McTiernan realized that allowing the camera to move freely during the extensive interrogation sequences throughout the film would give these otherwise static expository moments some fluidity, a sense of movement, and a sense of the screws tightening on the characters in the story.

The movie also continually exposes itself as something different than what the audience had expected from one moment to the next. The plot developments pile on top of each other relentlessly as Travolta and Nielsen's characters try and find the truth, so McTiernan felt if they acknowledged the absurdity of the story with their own sighs and gasps and throwaway comments it would indemnify the audience with the central characters.

Originally, *Basic* was intended to be a PG-13 thriller. The stipulation was even in McTiernan's contract. Then Samuel L. Jackson arrived on set and began dressing down his platoon of soldiers using more than enough foul language to give the film an R rating. McTiernan loved the scene as it was, so he called the studio and tried to convince executives to let the film go with the R rating. They were apprehensive, but once Sam Jackson turned on his charm executives were convinced the R rating would make for a more authentic finished product.

26. Basic

The biggest logistical issue with *Basic* was the rain. From beginning to end, except for the opening shots of the Panama Canal with Nielsen's voiceover, it would be raining. McTiernan planned on the constant rain becoming its own character in the story, intensifying the film's strangeness. But rain, especially in the convoluted jungle sequences, became a headache because characters had to shout their lines to make them audible over the showers. The shouting still was not enough sometimes, so the Automated Dialogue Replacement (ADR) in postproduction would take a little more time than normal.

The editing process would also be rather extensive for *Basic*. McTiernan and editor George Folsey, Jr., knew the story needed to fit together like a puzzle, with repetitive visual cues and strategically placed hints and tests for the audience. The jungle scenes were easy to time-stamp with the same grenade explosion, which let the audience know they were back at the beginning of the flashback, only from a different perspective. The heavy exposition scenes had their own challenge when it came to character names, which were thrown at the audience before they would have an opportunity to put a name to a face. McTiernan and Folsey knew repetition was the best way to make sure everyone could figure out who was whom in the shortest amount of time.

Basic opened March 28, 2003, after wrapping almost twelve months earlier, to widespread indifference. Critics were not particularly kind to the storyline, which appears to undermine itself time and time again as plot twists happen in the middle of other plot twists. The screenplay manipulates the audience too many times, eventually rendering the entire story leading up to the last five or ten minutes completely unnecessary.

John Travolta performs admirably as the wiry DEA agent; it's clear he is having fun in the role. And Connie Nielsen is a strong presence alongside Travolta, even if she does struggle to consistently nail down her thick Florida accent. In fact, all the actors turn in solid work here, and McTiernan's direction in concert with cinematographer Steve Mason and the editing with George Folsey, Jr., pieces together a riveting thriller on the surface. The problem with *Basic* lies in the machinations of James Vanderbilt's screenplay, a muddled parade of twists and turns that work to fool the audience rather than carry them along through an intriguing story of double-crosses. And those double-crosses don't even matter in the end.

It is easy to see why McTiernan was drawn to a story about distrust and paranoia at this stage in his career; his work and his personal life were beginning to crumble under the weight of controversy and contentious relationships. He continued to butt heads with studio executives and producers, and while his personal life was spread thin with court cases and a new family, *Basic* became an avatar for McTiernan's own inner turmoil, a messy thriller built on strange, unexplained events and pulsing with paranoia. In that sense, *Basic* is an interesting portrait of a great director who seemed to be losing his way through forces both external and internal.

Basic opened fourth at the box office in March of 2003, with $11.5 million. It ended its feeble domestic run with just over $26 million, roughly half of its budget.[4] Another failure added to McTiernan's ledger had put his career on life-support. Little did he know *Basic* would likely be the last feature film he would make in his career.

Part VIII

Pellicano

27

The Pellicano Problem

Two thousand three may not have gotten off to the best start for McTiernan with the failure of *Basic*, but like so many times in the past when bad news hit his life, a silver lining appeared. John and his fiancée, Kate Harrington, celebrated the birth of their first son, John "Jack" Clarence McTiernan, and on July 19 of that year the couple married.

Unfortunately, the marriage did not last long. The two first separated in 2005; if that was not enough of a headache, McTiernan's divorce hearing with Donna Dubrow was still ongoing in the courts. Finally, in October of 2005, the Dubrow divorce proceedings came to a close and the judge ruled that McTiernan's earnings as a director were not considered "goodwill value," meaning he did not have to split the income he made as a filmmaker with his ex-wife.[1]

McTiernan assumed the door on his relationship with Donna Dubrow had been closed. But that door would be opened again. His real legal problems had not even begun.

Anthony Pellicano was born March 22, 1944, in Chicago. He grew up in the suburb of Cicero, Illinois, former home of the infamous mobster Al Capone. Seduced by the organized crime that peppered the history of his childhood neighborhoods, Pellicano began to fashion himself as an entrepreneurial mobster. He worked as a bill collector in Chicago, fine-tuning his intimidation skills before he decided to start his own business as a private investigator. In 1977, he found the perfect client to launch his career as a Hollywood hotshot: Elizabeth Taylor.

Taylor's third husband, theater and film producer Michael Todd, had died in a plane crash in 1958 and his body was buried in a cemetery outside Chicago. In the summer of '77, Todd's grave was discovered vandalized and his remains stolen. The case had Chicago police stumped, but not Pellicano, who used his questionable mob ties to hunt down the location of Todd's remains. He beat the police to the punch—allegedly due to the fact that he and Todd had similar connections to the Chicago organized-crime scene—and returned Todd's remains, much to Taylor's relief. The entire situation was shrouded in underground dealings and mystery, questions Pellicano never answered once he completed the investigation. Regardless of the means by which Pellicano succeeded, the actress was pleased with the efficient work; a few years later she brought him to Los Angeles to meet some of her powerful Hollywood friends.[2]

One such friend was Howard Weitzman, a Los Angeles attorney who hired Pellicano in 1983 to help him defend his client, carmaker John DeLorean, who had been charged with trying to traffic fifty-five pounds of cocaine inside one of his iconic sports cars. Pellicano exposed fraudulent tapes the prosecution were trying to pass off as evidence; the case was eventually dismissed, and Pellicano had made his mark on the West Coast.[3]

Pellicano called himself a dozen different things when he first arrived in Los Angeles. He was an aspiring actor, a screenwriter, an expert in martial arts, and a stellar private investigator, depending on whomever was listening. He opened his private-investigation firm and immediately began taking in the highest of high-profile clients.

He shoehorned his way into A-list circles in Hollywood, where it became clear he had little ambition to act or write for the movies. Anthony Pellicano was an intimidator and a snoop who soon began taking vital surveillance jobs for Bert Fields, a Los Angeles attorney with a long list of celebrity clients. Fields had Pellicano spying on celebrities like Sylvester Stallone and Nicole Kidman, while Pellicano was making inroads with agents and producers at power lunches and in meetings on the top floors of Hollywood studio office buildings. Super-agent Michael Ovitz became a Pellicano client, as did producer Brad Grey who, at one point, wanted to make Pellicano's life story into an HBO series.

Spying on celebrities was not the only skill Pellicano brought with him to Hollywood. He also became an expert at covering up indiscretions for high-profile clients, burying secrets, and making scandals go away through intimidation and blackmail. He was known to carry a Louisville Slugger in the trunk of his car, and he frequently worked for Hollywood elites and attorneys who had certain problems with talkative witnesses and pushy journalists looking to expose controversy. He became a "fixer" for the Hollywood elite.

27. The Pellicano Problem

In 1993, Michael Jackson's legal defense team hired Anthony Pellicano to investigate the child-abuse claims that had been leveled against the King of Pop. During his time on the case he allegedly uncovered some disturbing information regarding Jackson and the several children he brought to his Neverland Ranch in California. Rather than expose these details, he simply removed himself from the investigation and kept his mouth shut. He was a stickler for privacy.

One of Pellicano's most notable victories was allegedly discrediting an unnamed male wrestler who claimed to have had a sexual relationship with Tom Cruise. Through his surveillance and intimidation techniques, Pellicano exposed the wrestler as a fraud and cleared Cruise of the scandal before it ever leaked to the mainstream media. That was not his only interaction with Cruise, who allegedly hired the P. I. to investigate Nicole Kidman during the power couple's very public divorce.

It was also rumored that Pellicano was one of the first people to discover Arnold Schwarzenegger's affair and subsequent lovechild with his maid, Patty Baena, in 1997 before any of the information became public many years later. Pellicano accumulated dirt on dozens of major Hollywood players, but never exposed a single one. As criminal as his enterprises may have been, Pellicano lived by a firm code: never roll over on your clients or your friends.

Speaking of codes, Anthony Pellicano was somewhat obsessed with the mob lifestyle and the influence it had on pop culture. Gangster films had found new life in the 1970s with the help of Francis Ford Coppola and Martin Scorsese, and the genre was soon woven into the tapestry of the country. Pellicano and his fourth wife, Katherine, would often spend their nights at home in the late '90s watching David Chase's groundbreaking mob series *The Sopranos* on HBO, or one of the *Godfather* films on video. He named his autistic son Luca, after Don Corleone's loyal foot soldier Luca Brasi (Lenny Montana) in the original film.

Pellicano's obsession with organized crime continued as he began to fashion himself as an atypical Southern California mob boss. In 2002, he may have pushed his mobster guise too far, when the FBI got wind of an intimidation plot against *Los Angeles Times* journalist Anita Busch. Busch had written scathing reports on the fledgling career of agent (and Pellicano friend) Michael Ovitz over the previous few years. She was in the thick of a new story about the mob's ties to action star Steven Seagal when she found out the hard way that a few people in Hollywood wanted this story to vanish.

One day, in the middle of this investigation, Busch went out to her car to find the window had been smashed in and a dead fish was left on the ground next to the driver's side door. There was a note on the car as well, attached to a single red rose, with only one word scribbled on it: STOP.[4]

An understandably shaken Busch contacted the FBI, who began investigating the incident. Several early signs pointed to Anthony Pellicano and his underling Alexander Proctor, a career criminal and enforcer who had ties to drug smuggling and Russian organized crime. But the investigators needed a reason to raid Pellicano's agency. That's when the FBI and prosecuting attorneys acquired the services of Daniel Patterson.

Unlike Pellicano and his crew, Daniel Patterson had no interest in Hollywood. A Temple City, California native and grandfather of eleven children, sixty-four-year-old Patterson had been married to his second wife for thirty years and lived a nondescript life in the suburbs. He rarely even saw movies at the theater, let alone got tangled up in the shady underground dealings of the Hollywood elite. There was one catch to this otherwise mundane existence: Daniel Patterson had been convicted of at least three felonies spanning several years, the most recent being a fraud charge where he was caught attempting to steal gold and silver from various manufacturers. These felonies forced him to become an informant for a prosecutor named Daniel Saunders in order to avoid time behind bars.

Saunders and the agents in charge of the Busch investigation pressed Patterson into meeting with Pellicano and recording their conversations. He met up with Alexander Proctor first, spinning a lie about how he wanted to get into the drug-running business. But Proctor was confident of his criminal enterprise, and needed little motivation to talk about his work. Proctor and Pellicano had grown more confident over the years, more boastful of their enterprises, and being able to show someone like Patterson the ropes tapped directly into Proctor's ego.

Eventually, Proctor's big mouth got Patterson into Pellicano's Sunset Boulevard office, a room crowded with monitors and televisions and elaborate recording gadgets. Using a microphone taped inside the lapel of his shirt, Patterson produced four audio recordings of his conversations with Proctor and Pellicano, who let enough information slip in Patterson's company that the prosecutors had the information they needed to obtain a warrant and move in on the private detective.

In the 2002 raid, federal agents uncovered a small cache of illegal plastic explosives, grenades, and a small arsenal of various weapons, all of which Pellicano claimed belonged to a motorcycle gang. The agents also unearthed a mountain of encrypted tapes, computer files, and transcripts of recorded conversations made surreptitiously through wiretaps set up all across Southern California. Pellicano had used vulnerable phone company employees to get his way into telephone junction boxes, where he could install taps that were directly tied in with switchboards operating the whole telephone grid in the area. He could pick and choose whom he wanted to listen to, and when; because this was the early 2000s, everyone still used landlines for the majority of their telephone conversations.[5]

The raid and investigation subsequently exploded into allegations of intimidation, bribery, identity theft, and just about anything else you could imagine in a criminal enterprise as far-reaching and powerful as the work of Anthony Pellicano. The media pounced, and the Justice Department responded, claiming this investigation might bring down Hollywood. Michael Ovitz was one of many high-profile Hollywood elites to be dragged into the fray, and his involvement with Pellicano would prove fatal to his already anemic Hollywood career.

In 2003, Pellicano pled guilty to the illegal explosives charge, which garnered him thirty months behind bars at Big Spring Federal Correctional Institute in Big Spring, Texas. He served his time and was on the verge of being a free man once again in 2006 when prosecutors re-indicted him, this time for the wiretapping and bribing of law-enforcement officials for access to confidential records.[6]

When this whole investigation began back in 2002, after the raid on Pellicano's office on Sunset Boulevard, the agents and federal prosecutors stirred up rumors that some of the biggest and best-known celebrities and power players in Hollywood would fall under the weight of exposed illegal activities, of which Pellicano had proof. The news would rock not only Hollywood, it would bring the entire industry to its knees. Names like Tom Cruise, Nicole Kidman, Michael Jackson, and Demi Moore were casually thrown around in the news as having ties to Pellicano. This scandal would, according to the Justice Department, reshape the entertainment industry.

But by 2006, while the investigation had delivered the goods on Anthony Pellicano, a handful of his closest collaborators, and the far-reaching tentacles of his illegal enterprise, the windfall of elite superstar names was failing to materialize. Most of this was because Pellicano himself refused to roll over on people the way the FBI had anticipated. Scrambling to find more names to attach to their case, which was effective but not quite as incendiary as they had promised, Daniel Saunders turned his attention to the relationship between Pellicano and John McTiernan.

McTiernan had been spending the last couple of years at his Wyoming ranch. He had not made another movie after the back-to-back failures of *Rollerball* and *Basic*. The court case involving his neighbors, the Scotts, and the conflict over water rights regarding irrigation had been settled, with McTiernan winning another court case.

In 2005, McTiernan was working with UBISOFT, the video-game company, supervising a video-game adaptation of *Die Hard*. He was also mulling over an unnamed action film, which took place primarily aboard an airplane. But in February of 2006, a phone call would interrupt the rest of his life.

It was around dinnertime on February 13, 2006, when the phone rang at McTiernan's Wyoming home. McTiernan answered, and the voice on the other end of the line claimed to be an FBI agent inquiring about his relationship with Anthony Pellicano. Divorce attorney Dennis Wasser had, at McTiernan's request, hired Pellicano to tap the phones of Donna Dubrow back in 1998. That was made clear in the raid on Pellicano's office; but the agent was not calling about the Dubrow wiretap.

The agent asked McTiernan if he had personally hired Pellicano in 2000 to tap the phones of Charles Roven, the *Rollerball* producer whom McTiernan suspected of sabotaging the film. McTiernan denied ever hiring Pellicano to spy on Roven, after which he hung up the phone. Two weeks later, armed with the recordings of Pellicano and McTiernan allegedly discussing tapping Roven's phones, the FBI arrived at the ranch with an arrest warrant. McTiernan was charged with illegal wiretapping and lying to a federal agent.

On the advice of his attorney, Olivier Diaz, McTiernan pled guilty to lying to federal agents in April of 2006. But then he decided to switch out legal representation, and in September of that same year his new counsel, Henry Hockeimer, convinced him to withdraw the guilty plea. He did so on the claim that Diaz had given him bad advice. Initially, the judge declined McTiernan's request to withdraw his plea, sentencing him to four months in prison. McTiernan appealed this decision, and in October 2008 the sentence was vacated and McTiernan was allowed to withdraw his guilty plea. He made the withdrawal official on February 24, 2009.

This would prove to be a costly decision, one that might have upset one prosecutor in particular, someone who clearly had a personal vendetta against the director.[7]

27. The Pellicano Problem

Daniel Saunders, like so many young dreamers across the country, came to Hollywood with his sights set on fame. Saunders wanted to be a screenwriter, and he arrived in California with senior thesis in tow, a script titled "The Death of William Shakespeare." His stage play did manage to land a small run at a local theater, but it never made any waves in the industry. It did not open any doors for Saunders, so he put his writing career on hold and decided to try his hand at acting.

Saunders acquired a talent agent named Jack Scagnetti, a small-time scout who specialized in getting his clients bit parts and minor supporting roles. Allegedly, Scagnetti sent all of his clients on bulk audition runs for two different films: the first was *Die Hard*; the second, *The Hunt for Red October*. Saunders did not get a role in either film, though it is unclear as to whether he went to these auditions since there is no paper trail. Odds are, unless he was out of town or otherwise incapacitated, Saunders did.

While he tried his hand at acting for a few more years, landing small roles in soap operas and minuscule stage plays from time to time, Daniel Saunders eventually came to terms with the fact that he was not going to be a star. Thankfully, he had a Princeton education to fall back on, so he enrolled in U. C. Berkeley law school and eventually found his way into the Century City law firm.

Saunders found more success as a lawyer and quickly joined the United States Attorney's Office as a prosecutor in the organized-crime division. And then, in 2002, the Anthony Pellicano case fell into Saunders's lap, where he spotted a certain name from his past tied to the illegal wiretapping scandal. Maybe Saunders saw an opportunity for vengeance on John McTiernan, who had played a part in his acting career ending before it had ever truly begun. That, at least, became a possibility floated out in the media from the McTiernan camp.[8]

The U.S. Attorney's Office cited the rift between McTiernan and Charles Roven on the *Rollerball* set as the motive for McTiernan's contact with Pellicano. There was, after all, the fire on the locker-room set in Canada, and there were more than enough whispers about arguments between the two men over the direction of the film; there was also a great deal of confusion. When the trial originally began back in 2006, several people did not recall any consternation between the producer and director.

The U.S. Attorney's Office announced their case against McTiernan on April 3, 2006, and people close to both sides were bewildered. Kate Harrington, who was still technically married to McTiernan at the time of the accusations (though the two had separated the previous year), was also the costume designer on the *Rollerball* set. She pointed out in her interview with *Deadline*'s Nikki Finke that the report of a contentious relationship between her estranged husband and Roven was something she never witnessed on set.⁹ In her recollections, there had been no major arguments and that the two men had a solid working relationship.

Now that the case had been re-opened and all prior indictments vacated, Saunders put forth a plan to not only indict McTiernan once again on lying to federal agents, but he was ready to add a charge of perjury stemming from McTiernan's decision to withdraw his guilty plea.

Rather than sit around his Wyoming home and wait on a new indictment to come down, John McTiernan began his own investigation. He turned his attention to an unlikely place, and would begin assembling material for a documentary on an unlikely subject: Karl Rove.

28

The Political Prosecutions of Karl Rove

John McTiernan was certain Daniel Saunders and his team of prosecutors would re-indict him on the charges of lying to a federal agent. But he did not sit idly by; McTiernan began his own digging into the Anthony Pellicano case, why it actually happened in the first place, and who may really have been behind it all. The investigation pointed him to some unusual places, and directed him to positions in the highest offices of American government.

Pellicano, meanwhile, had been found guilty on seventy-six of his seventy-seven charges ranging from illegal wiretaps to conspiracy and racketeering in 2008. He had just begun serving his fifteen-year prison sentence in Big Spring, Texas, when McTiernan was taking his own fight against the legal system into some surprising directions.

McTiernan's research unearthed a complicated web of alleged conspiratorial scheming, beginning as early as 1992. During Bill Clinton's initial presidential campaign, an actress and model named Gennifer Flowers came forward claiming to have had a twelve-year relationship with the then Arkansas governor. Allegedly, Hillary Clinton hired Anthony Pellicano to try and discredit—and possibly intimidate—Gennifer Flowers so she would not obstruct the Clintons' path to the White House. Pellicano claimed to do work for the Clintons throughout their time in the White House, including background searches on Monica Lewinsky when the scandal involving the former intern and the president exploded in the late 1990s.[1]

And then, in 2002, as the power in Washington, D.C., transitioned to the George W. Bush administration, Pellicano was abruptly indicted on wiretapping charges. He may have been tied to the Anita Busch intimidation plot, which drew the attention of the FBI, but McTiernan's research into Pellicano's early relationship with the Clintons was the start of a snowball that would build in size and scope as the director dug even deeper.

McTiernan found a 2007 report compiled by Donald Shields and John Cragan, both professors of communication at the University of Missouri, which detailed how the Justice Department's prosecutions of elected officials from 2002 through 2006 had disproportionately profiled and charged Democrats, many times for erroneous or minor infractions. And as he continued his research, he discovered that none other than Karl Rove was behind this biased legal crusade against left-leaning officials.

Karl Rove had been in politics since the late 1960s. In 1972, he joined the Richard Nixon presidential campaign, which was a success despite the growing mistrust surrounding the Republican incumbent. Later in the decade, Rove found his way south to Texas, and into the good graces of the Bush political family. He worked with George H. W. Bush during his presidential campaign and, eventually, became well known as the architect of George W. Bush's successful gubernatorial campaigns in Texas before becoming a senior advisor to President Bush in 2001 following the controversial 2000 presidential election victory. Known for his divisive, manipulative political tactics, Rove immediately ascended to one of the most powerful positions in the Bush administration. He was the man behind the scenes, a shadowy figure pulling strings in government and media, working diligently to keep the Republican Party in control for the foreseeable future. According to McTiernan's research, he was working to create a permanent Republican majority in the United States by systematically destroying the credibility and careers of elected Democrats across the country. McTiernan saw himself, then, as collateral damage when Anthony Pellicano's name was dragged into Rove's crusade.[2]

This was the jumping-off point for McTiernan, who was inspired to do what he knew best: make a film. Only McTiernan's reputation had been significantly tarnished with the ongoing ties to Pellicano and the impending indictment; he had no way to produce a documentary film with the help of a studio or a union crew. He decided to put the documentary together on his own.

McTiernan did the legwork, piecing together dozens upon dozens of interviews with state legislators, circuit judges, city mayors, and all manner of lower-level elected officials from across the country who had found themselves the target of the Justice Department. According to the interviewees, threats and intimidation were often included with these fatuous

28. The Political Prosecutions of Karl Rove

charges, and McTiernan sought to give a platform to as many of the victims as possible.

According to McTiernan's documentary, of the roughly seven hundred elected officials investigated by the U.S. Justice Department from 2002 to 2008, 87 percent of them were Democrats. It could not be a mere coincidence. Even the rare Republicans who were indicted during this time were on their way out of office, retiring, or tied firmly to the old money in the country; any legal issues would serve as mere distractions for these indicted Republicans as they permanently left their offices to live comfortably.

McTiernan put the interviews together using black-and-white footage and an ominous, pulsating musical score. He narrated the entire film, a fifty-minute barrage of information that built a complicated web of conspiracy and misdeeds by Karl Rove and his legal soldiers. Even though the documentary is under an hour in length, the exposition and the amount of information is enough to fill a textbook of possible corruption in the highest offices of the American government.

There was not a studio in sight willing to distribute *The Political Prosecutions of Karl Rove*, so McTiernan built a (now defunct) website and released the film on his own. But he did his fair share of interviews in April 2009 to discuss and promote the film, including an interview with Michael Cieply of the *New York Times*, wherein he voiced his concerns that this documentary would only hurt his impending legal case.[3] He also appeared on *The Young Turks*, one of the largest online news shows. Cenk Uygur and Ana Kasparian are the hosts of *The Young Turks*, and despite their claim that they are an independent news organization, their politics lean decidedly left.

With McTiernan's appearance on *The Young Turks*, it was clear his legal issues and the research he had conducted to put together his documentary had shifted his political affiliations from moderate, fiscal conservative to something undefined, something decidedly more liberal.

Shortly after releasing the documentary, prosecutors re-indicted McTiernan for lying to the FBI. They also added a second charge to his ledger, claiming his initial guilty plea and subsequent withdrawal qualified as perjury. Just like that, McTiernan's legal battle was re-ignited, and it would last for another four years.

29

Keep Moving

John McTiernan kept moving forward while a small team of lawyers battled on his behalf. In November 2009, he served as the jury president at the 6th Annual Amazonas Film Festival in Manaus, the Capital of Amazonas in Brazil. Notable winners of the festival included Warwick Thornton's Best Film winner, *Samson & Delilah*, and the audience prizewinner, John Hillcoat's adaptation of Cormac McCarthy's novel *The Road*.[1]

McTiernan continued his film festival work in January 2010 when he was again a jury president; this time he presided over the Gérardmer International Fantastic Film Festival, a science-fiction and horror festival held in Vosges, France. A month later, he was invited by the Directors Guild of America and the African American Steering Committee to celebrate the life and career of Bill Duke, who had played Mac in *Predator*. Carl Weathers, Dillon from *Predator*, was also in attendance. McTiernan was one of a handful of peers who spoke about Duke's accomplishments as an actor and humanitarian.[2]

The tour through film-festival circuits and tributes to actors in his past should have been a terrific time for John McTiernan, and a great way for the then fifty-nine-year-old legend to ease into his later years and possibly even continue his career behind the camera if the opportunity came his way. But opportunities were not coming his way, because the court case hung over him. He was too hot for studios to handle, his future too up in the air for anyone to throw a sizeable budget for a movie in his direction; the legal battles combined with the weak performances of his last two films had dried up the well.

The summer of 2010 was a mess for McTiernan in the courts. Evidence had emerged from Pellicano's collection of recordings in the form of a tape recording, in which the director and private investigator can be

29. Keep Moving

heard discussing the tapping of Roven's phones for a fee of $50,000. This revelation flew in the face of the claim from Kate Harrington back in 2006, when the case first began, that McTiernan and Roven had a good working relationship. Apparently, something had gone awry between the two. There was nothing of consequence in the tape recordings beyond a simple discussion between the two men, although a brief investigation had shown McTiernan *did* pay for Pellicano's services the second time around.

McTiernan and his legal-defense team tried to suppress the recordings from court records in June, but they had a tough time getting any cooperation from District Judge Dale Fischer, who was the judge the first time around when McTiernan pled guilty and promptly withdrew said plea. Fischer had since grown impatient with McTiernan, and she felt the director was not showing any remorse for his transgressions (an opinion she voiced in the courtroom), so she promptly denied the request to keep the recordings out of evidence.

In July, with the tapes of McTiernan's conversations part of the record, the director pled guilty on all counts. Three months later, on the suggestion of the prosecutors, he was sentenced to one year in a federal prison, but Judge Fischer added three years' probation and a $100,000 fine. It was her own little embellishment to the case.[3]

McTiernan's attorneys immediately appealed the decision and he was released on bond, pending said appeal. They turned their attention to those recordings between McTiernan and Pellicano, which they felt should never have been allowed as evidence. In fact, the tapes of their conversations might have discussed wiretapping Roven's calls, and what something like that might cost, and money was exchanged, but there was never any evidence that Pellicano actually went through with the job and tapped any of Roven's communications. It was as if Anthony Pellicano never went through with his end of the bargain.

There was also the issue of Judge Dale Fischer, whom McTiernan and his defense argued should have recused herself from the case after certain comments she made regarding McTiernan's character and his lack of remorse when she initially denied suppression of the tapes.[4]

In the midst of this intense legal battle, McTiernan was still trying to get another directing project off the ground. Perhaps it was a means to distract, or perhaps it was more pragmatic: the bills were stacking up and the steady income had stopped after *Basic* more than seven years prior. The only thing left as far as annual income were residual checks, which were sizeable, but not enough to stay afloat. In the years following *Basic*, McTiernan had a number of potential projects in the pipeline, all of which were stymied after his arrest in 2006.

There was "The Camel Wars," a film written by Robert Tobin, about an Iraqi American citizen who is sent to war in 2004.[5] Shortly after the Pellicano story broke, McTiernan signed on to direct "Deadly Exchange," the story of a terrorist hunting down the FBI agents responsible for his father's death.[6] And there was "Run," a chase film involving an Interpol agent. Thomas Jane was one name attached to star.[7] All of these potential projects fell apart when McTiernan was unable to secure a Film Production Completion Bond, which was basically an insurance policy used to guarantee a producer can finish the film in question. As his legal fight dragged on, the invoices accumulated and the income remained stagnant.

In September of 2010, after he filed his appeal, McTiernan signed on with a small production company named FilmEngine to direct "Shrapnel," based on a screenplay written by an unknown young writer named Evan Daugherty.[8] The story revolved around two war veterans who begin hunting each other in the deep woods. John Travolta was attached to star, and somehow, despite the legal issues, funding for the project fell into place when McTiernan hopped on board. The shoot was scheduled for the following spring, but any prospective scheduling depended on McTiernan winning his court appeal.

In 2012, McTiernan took time out of his tempestuous journey through the American legal system to marry his fourth wife, Gail Sistrunk. The two had been dating for about a year, and Sistrunk was proving to be a determined ally in McTiernan's corner as his battle raged on.

On August 20, 2012, the Ninth U.S. Circuit Court of Appeals denied McTiernan's most recent request that the tapes be stricken from the record; they also denied a request regarding Judge Fischer's proposed recusal from the case. The circuit court did, however, allow McTiernan to submit his appeal to the U.S. Supreme Court, his final option for salvation.

In January of 2013, the U.S. Supreme Court declined to hear his case, and John McTiernan was out of options. "Shrapnel" was dead, and now McTiernan had to come to terms with the fact that he would be going to jail.

30
Inmate #43029-112

Tucked away in the southeastern corner of South Dakota, along the banks of the Missouri River, lies Yankton. It is a small town, with a population of roughly fifteen thousand citizens. This quaint river town, built on steamboats traveling westward during the years of American expansion, would be the temporary home of John McTiernan when he surrendered to the authorities and was sent to the Yankton Federal Prison Camp on April 3, 2013. He was inmate number 43029–112.

The Yankton Prison Camp is a minimum-security penitentiary housing between four and five hundred male inmates at any given time. The atmosphere and amenities would never be confused with the bleak prison dungeons of Riker's Island or Alcatraz—the Yankton Prison Camp is typically noted as one of the country's coziest penitentiaries—it is nevertheless a massive sea change for someone who had spent the previous decades of his life directing feature films and spending his down-time on a 3,300-acre ranch in the vast openness of Wyoming.[1]

John McTiernan went from making upwards of $5 million per picture to accumulating a mountain of attorneys' fees. During this time he also struggled to come to terms with living in the confines of a South Dakota prison camp. It was a challenging adjustment at first, as it would be for anyone in his situation, and it was a month before Gail came to visit. The food supply was limited in prison; McTiernan had already shed twenty pounds in four weeks, and was pallid and barely recognizable to Sistrunk when she saw him. It would be a long year, but Sistrunk would continue the fight for him outside the walls of Yankton. McTiernan, meanwhile, would eventually summon new creativity behind bars, and find the inspiration to write again.

In the weeks leading up to McTiernan's imprisonment, Sistrunk and a few of McTiernan's powerful allies in the film industry began to rally behind what they felt was a blatant case involving abuses of power. In their minds this was a witch hunt, possibly spurred on by bitter vengeance from the Justice Department and the fervent desire of the FBI to nail a high-profile name to the Anthony Pellicano case when it was clear the true megastars of Hollywood were not going to be named in any indictments.

Even though Alec Baldwin and John McTiernan had rarely crossed paths after their collaboration on *The Hunt for Red October*, Baldwin got wind of the case and the jail sentence and felt a great injustice had been done. It was not necessarily that McTiernan was wholly innocent of any wrongdoing in Baldwin's opinion, which he voiced in the Michael Hastings article at Buzzfeed; it was more an issue of wasted resources on trumped-up charges, and it proved to Baldwin that the legal system could potentially get away with anything.

Samuel L. Jackson, who worked with McTiernan on both *Die Hard: With a Vengeance* and *Basic*, came to the director's defense as well. Jeremy Irons, Simon Gruber from *Vengeance*, also spoke out on his behalf. And then, mere days before McTiernan surrendered in South Dakota, a Twitter and Facebook page materialized with the title: "Free John McTiernan."

The social media pages were assembled in an unlikely place from an unexpected ally: France. Several French fans of McTiernan's work, and a handful of journalists in French newspapers, began investigating the beleaguered director's case on their own and came to the conclusion that he was railroaded into a conviction to justify all the time and money spent by the attorney's office. In only a few days, the page had accumulated more than two thousand likes, and the support from Jackson, Irons, directors Joe Carnahan and Brad Bird—both of whom credit *Die Hard* as their own career inspirations—and a number of friends in the industry helped increase this grassroots social media movement to try and free John McTiernan.[2]

McTiernan's wife, Gail, was another of his staunchest supporters. She went to Go Fund Me, one of the relatively new personal fundraising websites, to attempt to raise money for McTiernan's looming legal fees and possibly even set him free early, if the claims of prosecutorial misconduct were honored. At the very least, Gail could file another appeal to have the conviction stricken from his ledger. The fundraising effort did not take off as well as it should have, but Gail remained steadfast.

Finally, she saw some of the fruits of her labor in October 2013. The Ninth Circuit Court of Appeals granted McTiernan a certificate of appeal,

30. Inmate #43029-112

possibly getting the felony conviction stricken from his record; the appeal hearing would take place in January of the following year, in the tenth month of McTiernan's twelve-month sentence.

John McTiernan's weight loss was not the only change the director was going through during his time of incarceration. His thick brown hair had begun to gray a bit more, his eyes darkened, and his mind began to re-arrange itself. There was a range of emotion, from anger to resentment to eventual acceptance; and then there was observation.

Surrounding McTiernan were inmates who, like him, had been convicted on trumped-up charges. Only these were inmates without the resources to fight the good fight, as McTiernan had done for so many years. Many of these prisoners were young men of color who did not belong behind bars, but were pushed into the cycle of incarceration and forced to become part of the prison "system" thanks to furtive charges, often times revolving around something known as "ghost dope."

Criminal informants and undercover "snitches" will often estimate the quantity of drugs tied to a certain suspect, or how much of this weight could be connected to an individual facing potential prosecution. As these

Yankton Federal Prison Camp in Yankton, South Dakota, John McTiernan's place of incarceration for ten months, from 2013 to 2014 (Federal Bureau of Prisons website [bop.gov]).

informants stack their claims on top of one another, a concrete physical amount is then attached to the defendant in question in order for them to meet statutory minimums in a drug case. In other words, through the unreliable use of criminal deposition, many times from drug addicts and various untrustworthy criminal elements, prosecutors are allowed to send people to prison based on an amount of narcotics that are never admitted into physical evidence, and may have never existed at all. This, in a nutshell, is ghost dope.[3] The institution was rigged, especially against poor minorities in the United States, and McTiernan realized he was simply another spoke in the wheel of abuse of power, even though he had not been a marginalized member of society. Eventually, he began writing again.

McTiernan had not written a screenplay for any of his movies since *Nomads* back in the mid–1980s. But everything about penning a sequel to *The Thomas Crown Affair* made sense. Here he was, a man in prison with only his thoughts to occupy his time at night, able to focus on creating a terrific potential sequel to the most recent film in his catalogue that had been both critically and commercially successful. While Sistrunk worked diligently to get his appeal with the Ninth Circuit Court pushed through, McTiernan put together "Thomas Crown and the Missing Lioness."

For the plot, McTiernan conjured up a pair of entirely fictitious historical artifacts: two lion statues belonging to Nebuchadnezzar in 1100 B.C. From that origin, the statues made their way through the hands of Alexander the Great and Constantine as the powers of the world shifted, before they ultimately disappeared in the chasm of history. The story McTiernan was telling revolved around the two statues showing up unexpectedly at an auction.[4]

McTiernan's screenplay could have been seen as a serious attempt at a comeback once he was free; or, perhaps, it was more of a cathartic exercise for a man whose life and worldview had been permanently altered. Regardless, the writing recharged McTiernan's batteries, pulling him from the myopic doldrums of his first few months behind bars.

McTiernan's appeal to have the felony stricken from his record was denied by the Ninth Circuit Court in January, but there was good news just around the corner.

Tuesday morning, February 25, 2014, 328 days into his sentence, John McTiernan walked out of the federal prison camp in Yankton, a free man. He was lighter, a little grayer, and had an entirely new outlook on society. Gail shared the good news on the "Free John McTiernan" Facebook page,

30. Inmate #43029-112

much to the delight of the celebrities and fans that had been in his corner from the beginning.

McTiernan would remain under house arrest in Wyoming until his sentence officially ended on April 3, but it was still the beginning of a new chapter in his life. He would begin looking for work right away—some work would also come looking for him—but he carried a deep resentment from the sting of injustice. And, unfortunately, a new adversary would rear its ugly head while McTiernan tried to get his life back in order.

31

The Legal Mountain

The first order of business for McTiernan upon his release was to authorize his attorney, Hank Hockeimer, to file a formal complaint with the Justice Department's Office of Professional Responsibility. The complaint was another attempt to have the felony conviction stricken from his record because, according to the McTiernans and Hockeimer, John had not only been wrongly convicted; he had been charged with conduct that was not a crime to begin with.[1]

There had never been any concrete evidence presented in the courts that McTiernan had committed a crime. He had spoken to Pellicano, true; this was made clear on the recordings. Money was exchanged, but there were no recordings of Charles Roven. There was no concrete evidence that Pellicano had ever gone through with the wiretaps, despite the fact that he and McTiernan discussed the process at length.

McTiernan was on the offensive in the weeks and months following his release. In March, he invited CNN reporter Bill Weir out to Wyoming to discuss his prison term, the injustice he witnessed all around him, and his plans for moving forward. He was eager to get back to work, both because he wanted to and because he needed the money.

Back in October 2013, while in prison in South Dakota, McTiernan filed for Chapter 11 bankruptcy to protect his ranch from foreclosure. This proved to be a shrewd move, one that upset First Interstate Bank, which had tried to foreclose on the property earlier in the year in order to collect almost $6 million in loans against the ranch. These loans were used for improvements to the land and the residence. The McTiernans also turned down an offer to sell the ranch for $8 million in 2013, because they valued the property at no less than $10 million. McTiernan was still receiving upwards of $200,000 a month in residual paychecks from his films, but that money was leaving just as quickly as it came in. And it was no match for the liens against his property.

There was also a new lawsuit filed by Donna Dubrow. She discovered, during the Pellicano trial, that McTiernan hired the private investigator to tap her phones during their heated divorce proceedings. That lawsuit would be addressed in December; there were bigger fish for McTiernan to fry in the meantime, and there were a few interesting film projects coming his way that might just turn things around for him.

Hannibal Pictures would never be confused with the likes of Paramount or 20th Century–Fox. The small studio was founded in 1999 by Richard Rionda Del Castro, and it specialized in small, B-grade action pictures.[2] As the landscape of cinema was changing—avenues for video on demand projects and quick-turnaround movies with small budgets were increasing—Hannibal Pictures managed to grab well-known actors whose careers had seen better days.

Hannibal produced films like *The Big Bang* starring Antonio Banderas, *Giallo* with Adrien Brody, and *Partners in Action* with Armand Assante. None of these movies would have advertising budgets or marketing campaigns; their trailers would not be on any major networks. They were made to fill space and hopefully wind up in the black. It was the sort of studio where an actor like John Travolta could find work in 2014.

After *Basic*, Travolta's star continued to dim. His career became littered with dreadful comedies like the misguided *Get Shorty* sequel, *Be Cool*, the middle-aged biker buddy movie *Wild Hogs*, and forgettable remakes like *Hairspray* and *The Taking of Pelham 123*. In 2013, with his box-office power all but dissolved, he finally got around to making "Shrapnel," which had been planned with McTiernan before the director's life unraveled. Now, "Shrapnel" was called "Killing Season," and Mark Steven Johnson was the director. It co-starred Robert De Niro, who had his fair share of questionable film choices over the prior decade-plus. *Killing Season* was released directly to home video with only a handful of theatrical showings scattered across the country; it was resoundingly panned and then forgotten.

This sort of precipitous decline in Travolta's career is partly what brought him to Hannibal Pictures. He signed on to star in their new film, "Warbirds," a dogfighting action movie with aspirations to be the new *Top Gun*, but with CGI to create more intense, albeit computer-generated, aerial fight scenes. With Travolta on board and parts offered out to Queen

Latifah and *Jackass* star Johnny Knoxville, Hannibal approached McTiernan to direct.

Sensing an opportunity, any opportunity, to get his foothold as a director once again, McTiernan took the job. Hannibal offered him $1 million to direct, a marked difference from the $5 to $8 million he had once commanded. Nevertheless, McTiernan was back in the Hollywood machine (even if it was a fringe production company) taking extended meetings about "Warbirds" and sampling possible CGI for the substantial action set pieces. While all this was happening, Hannibal came to him with yet another project, this one in their Hannibal Classics division, and it would feature another former A-list star. And, like McTiernan, this actor had his own financial woes.

Nicolas Cage was a force to be reckoned with in the 1990s. He was an Oscar winner for his role as a suicidal alcoholic in *Leaving Las Vegas*; he was an action star with *Con Air* and *The Rock*; he was one of the hottest commodities in the industry, with the Coppola bloodline and an unmatched intensity anywhere in Hollywood.

And then, somewhere as the calendar flipped over the twenty-first century, Cage began to take on too many awful films to count. In his personal life, he was spending money faster than he was making it, his expenses creating a mountain of tax debt and forcing the actor to take any and every role he could to keep his head above water. He was the perfect type of former superstar Hannibal looked for to headline their B-pictures, like their new film, "Red Squad."

Written by Cam Cannon and Jorge Suarez, "Red Squad" is the story of a rogue DEA agent who squares off against drug lords at the Mexican border.[3] McTiernan agreed to shoot "Red Squad" on top of the work he was doing on "Warbirds"; he could figure out the complicated scheduling down the road.

The combination of McTiernan and Cage certainly felt serendipitous. Here were two once-celebrated masters of their craft, trying anything they could to get back on top, both taking projects for the money more than the prestige. "Red Squad" was green lit, so much so that a poster was created with McTiernan's name below the title.

McTiernan took the news of his two new film projects with him to Wyoming bankruptcy court for his hearing in the summer of 2014. With the bank trying to take over his ranch to pay off his debts, pushing the bankruptcy from a Chapter 11 filing over to a Chapter 7 so they could liquidate

31. The Legal Mountain

assets, McTiernan fired back with "Warbirds" and "Red Squad." He claimed the paycheck and residuals from these projects would be enough to begin paying off his creditors. Judge Peter McNiff was convinced by McTiernan's prospects, so he delayed conversion of the bankruptcy. It bought McTiernan more time to get his career back on the rails and begin paying off his debts.

Except the next year would not bring any relief; McTiernan's mountain of legal and financial issues continued to accumulate. The bank fought the judge's decision and was still set on liquidating his assets as soon as they could, because they did not buy into McTiernan's claim that the two movie projects would be enough to pay off his debts. The mortgage he had on his ranch with First Federal was accumulating upwards of $1,600 per day in interest, and as 2015 moved into the autumn months, McTiernan still had not sold.

If this had been McTiernan's only financial obligation, perhaps "Warbirds" and "Red Squad" could have been enough to reach a deal with First Federal. But the bank was merely the tip of the spear.

McTiernan had a few creditors. Aside from First Federal in Wyoming there was the issue with the Internal Revenue Service. They were coming for the roughly $110,000 McTiernan owed in back taxes from 2010, as well as taxes he had yet to file for 2012. Their invoice for McTiernan interfered with First Federal's plan to liquidate and pay their own debts; the snowball was flying downhill, getting larger and more destructive every day.[4]

A person from McTiernan's past had attached her name to the list of creditors as well: Donna Dubrow. She had discovered, through the Anthony Pellicano trial, that McTiernan hired the private investigator to spy on her during their mercurial divorce hearings. Armed with this information, Dubrow came for her pound of flesh, filing an invasion of privacy lawsuit against him and suing for the spousal support she never received.

The list was not complete quite yet. Enter James Jellis, the man who bought McTiernan's herd of Beefalo in 2010. The purchase was informal, a gentlemen's agreement settled with two cash payments. Jellis spoke to McTiernan about keeping the Beefalo on the ranch for the time being, and while the two parties initially agreed, their relationship deteriorated when discussion of a lease came up. The two could not agree on a price, and in the spring of 2011 McTiernan locked the gate to his ranch and did not allow Jellis access to the Beefalo. On top of this, McTiernan filed a lien

Part VIII: Pellicano

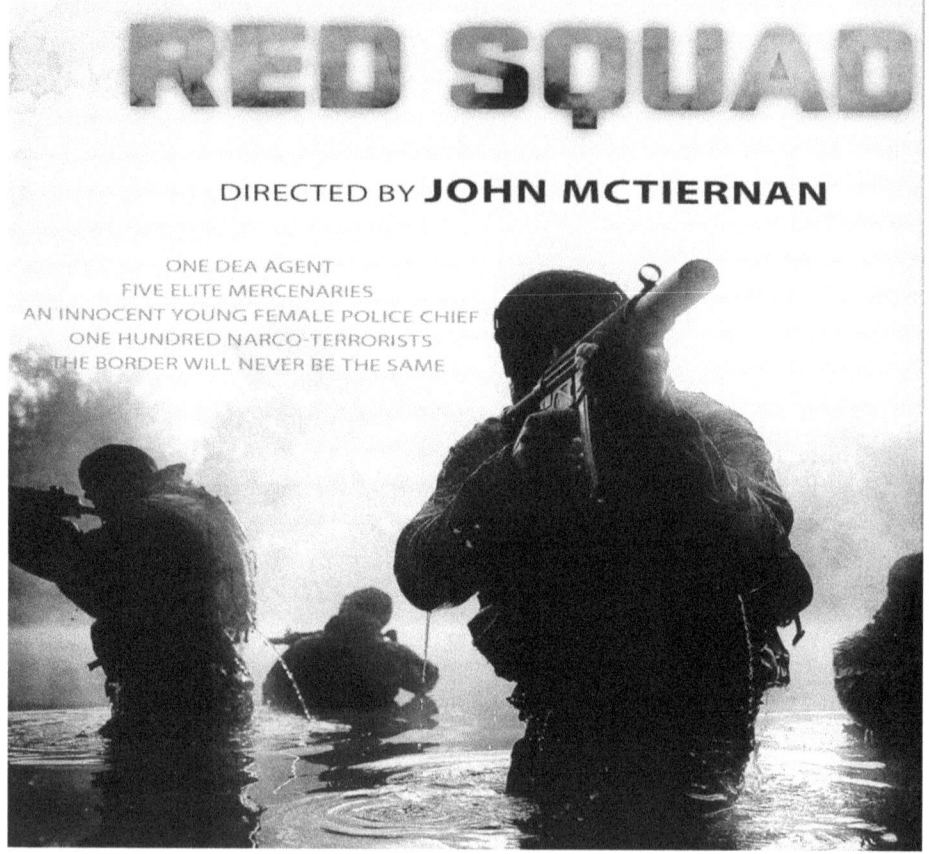

The poster from Hannibal Pictures, showing John McTiernan's name attached to "Red Squad."

against the herd, citing almost $24,000 in lease money owed. Jellis filed a counter complaint, and the bizarre land argument became simply another hurdle, and another headache, for John McTiernan.

With the murderer's row of creditors stacked up against him, his work prospects began to evaporate as well. "Warbirds" dissipated as if it had never gotten past the earliest stages of pre-production. In fact, there was hardly any mention of the film beyond what McTiernan said in his own words in the courtroom. These sorts of things happen, but this felt like an extreme disappearing act.

As for "Red Squad," it hung on for a little while. Cage was still

31. The Legal Mountain

attached, and Hannibal Classics kept the poster with McTiernan's name on it; but, eventually, "Red Squad" had to move on without McTiernan, who was far too embroiled in the courts to ensure he could complete a project. The directing duties were quietly handed over to a veteran cameraman and director of 2004's *Resident Evil: Apocalypse*, Alexander Witt. Nicolas Cage also bowed out, and everyone involved seemed to move on to other projects. Even with the new director on board, "Red Squad" is, as recently as 2017, still in some form of production limbo.

McTiernan had moved on as well, to a new bankruptcy hearing in October 2015. He had reloaded his gun with new projects that he was certain would save his career and pay off his debts.

First, McTiernan referenced his spec script for "Thomas Crown and the Missing Lioness." It remained his most desired—and probably most desirable—film project. Other movies he mentioned were less tangible than a sequel to his last successful film. "Venice Pier" was the working title of one of the potential projects. The other, "The Sleeping Dogs of Amagansett," was, ironically, set to have evil bankers as its villains.[5]

He laid out his plans, once again, to the courts. And he hoped it would be enough. It was not. All of these projects were speculative at best, with no substantive schedule or detail beyond what McTiernan and his attorney were presenting. The court was being asked to rely on intangible ideas which would allegedly become McTiernan's income.

In the early part of December 2015, the judge sided with First Federal and their plan to liquidate McTiernan's assets. The road had come to a close, here, with John McTiernan standing on the outside of his cherished Wyoming ranch, looking in. McTiernan's royalty checks would also go to First Federal, and he was given living expenses ($8,500 per month); because he knows no other way, McTiernan objected, and he fought until he had no more wiggle room. He was ordered to vacate the premises in Wyoming, and he was ordered by the courts to provide photographic evidence that he had packed his belongings and moved out.

As for those belongings, they would soon hit the road with John and Gail McTiernan. They wound up in a friend's guesthouse for a while, where McTiernan was pressed once again to find a foothold. To mount a comeback.

32

Burning Bridges

For John McTiernan, 2016 represented a new stage in his life, one he could never have predicted. His Wyoming ranch was ripped out from under his feet, his residuals were garnished, and he found himself a man without a permanent place of residence. What was more troubling, however, was the fact that he had no solid work prospects lined up.

His plan for "Thomas Crown and the Missing Lioness" dissipated in February, when MGM decided to green light a remake—which would be the third *Thomas Crown Affair* adaptation in the studio's catalogue—starring the young rising star from Creed, Michael B. Jordan. In fact, Jordan was cast in the lead before writers, a director, or producer ever attached their name. Even with the director's chair open, MGM showed little to no interest in hiring McTiernan for the job.

In May, Joe and Anthony Russo, known in the industry as the Russo Brothers, hopped on board the *Thomas Crown* remake as producers. The brothers had recently come off the successes of *Captain America: The Winter Soldier*, and *Captain America: Civil War*. Next in line was finding a director, and while the search dragged on, McTiernan never received a call. Instead, he went to France and started burning bridges.[1]

In June 2016, McTiernan attended the Sofilm Summercamp in the northwestern city of Nantes, France. The camp was a film festival of sorts, but also a place where creative minds from all over the landscape of cinema would gather to discuss film. The French journalism community had been behind John McTiernan from the beginning, so they welcomed him to the camp with open arms.

McTiernan took this opportunity, among journalistic allies, to do an interview with France's *Premiere* magazine. When the interview hit the Internet news cycle on July 3, it stirred up the angry masses. It was the first

32. Burning Bridges

time McTiernan's name had been a part of the news cycle for several months, but once again it brought with it negative connotations.

Early in the interview, McTiernan praised *Argo*, Ben Affleck's Oscar-winning hostage-rescue docudrama from 2012, as his favorite film of the past several years. It was the only film he commended in the interview; otherwise, he had some opinions on one of the most popular films of 2015, and he had plenty of opinions about the most popular current genre in Hollywood: the superhero movie.

Around the time John McTiernan received that fateful phone call at his Wyoming ranch in 2006, superhero movies were still somewhat of a children's game. Movies like Sam Raimi's *Spider-Man* and *Spider-Man 2* and Bryan Singer's *X-Men* franchise were major hits, and they injected some credibility into the genre. Christopher Nolan's take on Batman in 2005's *Batman Begins* was a step towards the maturation of superhero films. But at the same time, Ang Lee's muddled, existential 2003 take on *Hulk* was met with general confusion, Ben Affleck's attempt at *Daredevil* foundered, and the campy *Fantastic Four* movies had few, if any, redeeming qualities.

As a genre, superheroes were still hit or miss, and they did not necessarily guarantee big box office the way they do currently. The genre did not hit its stride until 2008, with the twofold success of Marvel's *Iron Man* and Christopher Nolan's second Batman film, *The Dark Knight*. From there, Marvel started what would be the first "shared universe" franchise, mining all their intellectual property for the foreseeable future; Nolan finished out his Dark Knight trilogy, and DC Comics almost immediately kicked off their own version of a shared universe, with their classic characters.

While John McTiernan fought for his freedom and his finances for the better part of a decade, the superhero genre became the biggest moneymaking machine in Hollywood. When *Premiere*'s François Léger asked McTiernan about the state of modern action movies, it was clear McTiernan was still harboring resentment from his prison situation and the trying previous decade of his life. His new, more radical political opinions snuck into his answer when he claimed fascists were responsible for superhero movies.

The entire genre, in McTiernan's opinion, was a way to tell children they could never accomplish their own goals. Kids would never be good enough on their own, and must rely on these superheroes, who have become big business in Hollywood, to save the day. Later in the interview, McTiernan had the same assessment of George Miller's *Mad Max: Fury Road*, dismissing it as a corporate product.

McTiernan also spoke to Léger about some of his work, the state of the action genre in more general terms, and philosophical discussions about the reach of cinema. Once the interview was published, however, none of these segments gained the sort of traction as the director's take on *Mad Max* and *Captain America*.

Something else happened in the world while John McTiernan was preoccupied: the combination of exploding social media, fan outrage based on childhood nostalgia, the mob mentality, and an endless abyss of blogs and news sites had completely altered the court of public opinion. Movies live and die on media coverage and Internet criticism in the modern era, a medium society had only begun to develop back when McTiernan was still directing feature films.

This new media world pounced on McTiernan's comments about superhero films and *Mad Max: Fury Road*, which is almost universally admired. The mob assembled, lit their torches, and charged hard at McTiernan, dismissing his entire interview as the opinions of a bitter has-been. None of the points were considered for a moment, they were simply spun into a nest of Internet rage.[2]

Once again, McTiernan was in the news cycle for all the wrong reasons.

33

The Comeback Kid?

John McTiernan fell out of the public eye in the summer of 2016, after the pushback he caught from his *Premiere* interview. He had burned too many bridges in Hollywood, and had become what *The Hollywood Reporter* described as "one of four figures so despised … they won't be welcomed back in the industry anytime soon."[1]

McTiernan turned his attention overseas, where he was not vilified. Finally, after roughly three months of radio silence, he emerged in China with news of a World War II film. According to McTiernan, it would focus on the Doolittle Raid.

The Doolittle Raid was one of the most pivotal moments in World War II and the Allied forces fight against the Japanese. American forces executed an air raid on Tokyo on April 18, 1942, revenge for the Pearl Harbor attack in 1941. The raid proved to both sides that Japanese metropolitan areas were vulnerable to attack, and it substantially reduced their military strength for the rest of the war. The leader of the raid was Lieutenant Colonel James Doolittle, hence the name. McTiernan's film allegedly would be more about the aftermath of the raid, and it would begin filming in 2017.[2]

Whether or not "The Doolittle Raid" film is underway in China remains a mystery. There has been no mention of the project since McTiernan brought it up in November 2016. Following the brief appearance in Shanghai, McTiernan went silent for another few months.

In the first week of January 2017, John McTiernan popped back up in the media, only this time the news was not negative. He had directed a one-minute, twenty-five second teaser trailer for *Tom Clancy's Ghost Recon: Wildlands*, a first-person shooter video game. In less than ninety seconds, John McTiernan reminded people he still had a grasp on action directing.

The trailer, titled *The Red Dot*, features a group of heavily tattooed gang members hiding out in an abandoned warehouse. The gang is sitting around a table, and a white cat lying nearby catches sight of a red laser dot traveling across the floor. Eventually, the red dot finds its way up to the gangsters, and they are taken out before they even have a chance to react. Cut to a hill hundreds of yards away, and two snipers react to their efficient assassinations.

It may not have been a tent pole, Hollywood action film; it wasn't even a Hannibal Pictures production. But it was a step in the right direction. It was the best bet for McTiernan, who had soured so many in the industry he needed the smallest window in which to sneak back. He worked with cinematographer Jeff Cronenweth, David Fincher's cameraman for *Fight Club*, *The Social Network*, *The Girl with the Dragon Tattoo*, and *Gone Girl*, on the trailer, and the opening tracking shot pushing in on the gang members is a prevalent technique in much of Fincher's work.

The trailer has some identifiable John McTiernan traits. He employs moving cuts, he keeps the camera fluid, and he has an acute eye for structure. What is most interesting about the trailer is the fact that the gunfire is minimal, a definite change of course in an advertisement for a first-person shooter, and there is a true sense of tension building in the first half. McTiernan takes the time, in a video-game commercial, to set up spatial geography between the gang members in the warehouse and the red dots searching for them. The assassination is explosive, and it pays off because of the trailer's ability to hold back.

With the *Ghost Recon* trailer, John McTiernan managed to subvert expectations once again, albeit on an incredibly smaller scale than his movies. Video-game trailers are regularly high-octane barrages of light and color and explosions; they do not take the time to do something as cinematic as build tension. But McTiernan does and, just like he did with *Predator*, *Die Hard*, and even *The Hunt for Red October*, he reshapes the idea of what a genre story can be. It isn't in the same stratosphere as those films, and it did not make any waves one way or another, but McTiernan still made the best of his first opportunity to direct in thirteen years.

UBISOFT, the company releasing *Ghost Recon* (which had also worked with McTiernan on a *Die Hard* video game in the mid–2000s), was pleased enough with his work on *The Red Dot* to have him direct a second trailer

33. The Comeback Kid?

for the same game. This one was called *Ruthless*, and it had many more moving parts than the first trailer. It takes place in multiple locations, and it runs over two minutes. This trailer is McTiernan growing more confident, being patient, taking in a few small breaths before his lungs get their strength and he tries to come back from the dead.

34

Nothing Lasts Forever

John McTiernan may never return to feature filmmaking. He is sixty-seven years old as of this writing (2017), and has spent the better part of the last twelve years with court cases, lawsuits, bankruptcy, a prison term, and a handful of alleged film projects that never developed beyond the discussion phase. If any of these movies did advance following a mention in court, they did so with another director behind the camera. He might never direct again, but once upon a time he *was* a great director; anything that happens in the future cannot destroy the past.

The tutelage of Ján Kadár during McTiernan's time at the American Film Institute proved to be serendipitous, given the way McTiernan would utilize the European style of filmmaking to reshape action cinema. Had McTiernan arrived at the AFI in another year, before or after Kadár's residence from 1975–1979, he may have been an entirely different filmmaker. Those lessons he learned on his own, sitting in dark theaters watching foreign films and paying little attention to the subtitles, could have been replaced with more conventional camera techniques with a different artist in residence. The foreign films helped create the building blocks of McTiernan's visual storytelling, and Jàn Kadàr only reinforced his sensibilities.

McTiernan did not intend to change the face of a genre when he landed *Predator*. He was eager and young, and just wanted to make a good movie; and, to be honest, *Predator* did not change things. It was a moderate hit, split almost down the middle by critics. Time has re-appraised *Predator*, however, and it has turned into a modern classic for genre enthusiasts. It has withstood the test of time, especially considering the fact that the middling 1990 sequel from Stephen Hopkins is rarely discussed or deconstructed.

34. Nothing Lasts Forever

Predator did not create the tidal wave of change; that was up next in McTiernan's career. *Die Hard* is one of history's seminal action films. It is lean and ferocious and funny and surprisingly emotional, and McTiernan handled the complexities of the story and the endless logistical headaches like a master. He grew even more confident in his abilities during *Die Hard*, commanding the set and dressing the part in jeans, heavy denim jackets, and tactical, epaulet shirts. He was always dressed ready to work, and he was a physical director, moving through scene blocking and ideas right alongside the actors.

McTiernan's tactile approach to filmmaking, undoubtedly borne from his pastoral upbringing on his mother's family farm, can be seen in *Die Hard*. This is not another burnished '80s action movie, but a sensational story about real human beings, grounded as much as possible in the real world. If there is any doubt of *Die Hard*'s reach across pop culture, just peruse the laundry list of films inspired by the self-contained setup of McTiernan's film.

The Hunt for Red October never made the sort of cultural impact as *Die Hard*, but it did reach the mass of Tom Clancy fanatics in 1990 and was the most critically well-received film of McTiernan's career at its time of release. His submarine picture was never intended to be an action movie, no matter how heavily that angle was marketed prior to release. This was a thriller of exposition, a challenging drama made for adult audiences, and it was a clear indicator that McTiernan had more to offer.

Hypothetically, if his career had simply ended after the trifecta of *Predator*, *Die Hard*, and *Red October*, or if he had inexplicably vanished for decades the way Terrence Malick did in back in 1978 after his back-to-back breakout films *Badlands* and *Days of Heaven*, John McTiernan would be considered an enigmatic legend to many fans of the action genre. His aura would burn bright and pure in the minds of pop-culture aficionados, and the rest of his life would be a mystery. Of course, that did not happen, and while there were promising moments in the 1990s, mistakes were made and trouble began to percolate.

Medicine Man is a competent film, an interesting art-house departure for McTiernan, but it never truly gains traction. Lorraine Bracco, as magical as she was in *Goodfellas*, as brilliant and reserved as she was in *The Sopranos*, holds the film back. She is grating and shrill, and, ultimately, a distraction. Even if it isn't the greatest film in McTiernan's catalogue, it was not bad enough to be the film that dried up his prospects in Hollywood.

McTiernan was obviously riding high when he hopped aboard the *Last Action Hero* ship, which steadily began to spring leaks and sank into a failure for the ages. This disaster was something much more damaging than any sort of mediocre *Medicine Man* film; it was real trouble for McTiernan, who witnessed first-hand the way big studios had completed the about-face from their *laissez-faire* approach in the 1970s to a more controlling regimen of moviemaking. The studio set the release date, handled the marketing, transformed the entire process into the same sort of "corporate product" McTiernan mentioned in the *Premiere* interview when discussing *Mad Max: Fury Road* some twenty years down the road. The trouble on *Last Action Hero* planted the first seeds of paranoia.

But John McTiernan is, and always has been, a fighter. *Last Action Hero* could have crushed another director. In fact, movies as calamitous as this *have* ruined careers. There was Michael Cimino's *Days of Heaven*, which just about ground his career to a complete halt. Elaine May never directed again after her infamous 1987 comedy *Ishtar*. Some directors scratched and clawed their way back after box-office and critical backfires: Kevin Reynolds shook off *Waterworld* to direct a few more films, including *The Count of Monte Cristo*, and John McTiernan returned with a vengeance.

Wading back into the world of John McClane was exactly what McTiernan needed in the wake of *Last Action Hero*. He and Bruce Willis seemed always to be in sync, developing their own language for the iconic character; this is the main reason why other directors in the franchise haven't quite had their finger on the pulse of John McClane. They do not understand the character. Willis and McTiernan shared a conservative outlook on the world, a rarity in Hollywood, and perhaps part of the reason they are able to tap into the psyche of a hardened New York cop.

As cathartic and re-invigorating as *Die Hard: With a Vengeance* was, *The 13th Warrior* brought McTiernan back to earth with a thud. But this one is not on McTiernan. *The 13th Warrior* is a strong film as it stands, but a messy one that has clearly been butchered by a dozen different opinions pulling the tone and the storytelling in opposing directions. Had McTiernan been given free rein on the film, and had he been allowed to complete his horror film the way he originally intended (after all, McTiernan joined the project back when it was still called "Eaters of The Dead"), there is no doubt it would have been markedly different, and a likely improvement. Instead, test audiences once again decided the fate of one of McTiernan's films.

34. Nothing Lasts Forever

Audience testing has been a part of Hollywood as far back as the 1930s. *The Wizard of Oz* was famously tested in 1939, and throughout the decades these small collections of varying demographics and backgrounds have shown to wield too much power in the decision-making process. Their collective opinion of a picture can change the face of said picture before wide release; perhaps the most notable alteration of the modern era was the decision to change the ending of *Fatal Attraction* after a negative test.

Audiences did not react well to the original *Fatal Attraction* ending, a darker and more symmetrical finale where Michael Douglas's adulterous husband is blamed for the death of Glenn Close's character once she commits suicide with a knife bearing his fingerprints. The studio pushed Douglas, Close, Anne Archer, and director Adrian Lyne to re-shoot the end with a more heroic, thrilling showdown, complete with the monster's return from the dead before finally being slain.

Fatal Attraction is the most notable casualty of test-audience interference. McTiernan was felled three times by test groups, and while the reactions may have been warranted for *Last Action Hero* and *Rollerball*, their misguided take on *The 13th Warrior* all but ruined the movie.

The delicious irony in McTiernan's favor here involves his other 1999 film. The re-shoots and postproduction of *The 13th Warrior* proved so arduous that McTiernan shot and finished *The Thomas Crown Affair* in that window, and released his breezy, vintage heist film a few weeks before *The 13th Warrior* stumbled into theaters. *Thomas Crown* more than doubled the final tally of the Viking adventure.

The Thomas Crown Affair would prove to be John McTiernan's last great hurrah in Hollywood. It was not his last film, of course, but the *Rollerball* disaster changed the course of McTiernan's future in every conceivable way. There is little to appreciate in *Rollerball*; it is a strange, choppy, manic work of poor quality from top to bottom. For all the infamous ups and downs of McTiernan's filmography, *Rollerball* is arguably the least redeemable misfire.

Basic might have been a forgotten spring release in 2003, and it *is* flawed; but it does not deserve the same amount of derision as *Rollerball*, or even *Last Action Hero*. *Basic* moves, whisked along on a current of paranoia and misdirection, and John Travolta is game for the role of the prickly, undermining investigator. The fatal flaw in the climax aside, the film showed that McTiernan still had command of his camera. Thankfully, he had abandoned the desire to create movies for "the MTV generation" the way he wanted in *Rollerball*, and *Basic* had the gravitas of a mature, sure-handed director in the chair.

It's a shame McTiernan was never given the chance to direct after *Basic*; there was enough good in the military thriller to warrant a shot at another solid comeback with a follow-up film. There is no doubt he had it in him in 2003, but the last decade-plus may have eventually, finally, taken him down.

A few things are clear: John McTiernan hired Anthony Pellicano to spy on his ex-wife Donna Dubrow during their divorce hearings. McTiernan also exchanged money with Pellicano to try and tap producer Charles Roven's communications during the contentious *Rollerball* shoot. But there was never any evidence that Pellicano ever went through with the surveillance on Roven. It does not excuse the fund exchange, but it at least exonerates McTiernan on the ultimate charge.

The way the investigation turned its attention to McTiernan reeks of conspiracy. Perhaps prosecutor Daniel Saunders always *did* harbor resentment for McTiernan after being turned down for roles in two films. It is farfetched, but not the most absurd idea. Regardless, the decision to call McTiernan at his Wyoming home and claim to be an FBI agent is a thin tactic, and should have been wholly combated by McTiernan's defense team. Initiating an eventual arrest warrant based on a phone call should not be able to stand up in court.

But it did, and McTiernan became the fall guy for a scandalous investigation that never bore the fruit of Hollywood superstar names the attorney's office had promised. He was a scapegoat; a notable enough name to ensure the investigation was not a total loss.

McTiernan's push back against the industry grew over the years, but it was not without merit. Columbia Pictures is to blame for the failures of *Last Action Hero*, plain and simple. Had Columbia given McTiernan the time he requested, and moved the release date by a few weeks, the meta-fictional adventure might have stood a chance in a summer movie season that had ample space for a teenage-leaning action film in the weeks after *Jurassic Park*. Ego was the only motivating factor when it came to Columbia's ultimate decision to wedge their tent pole right next to Spielberg and dinosaurs. It was this meddling that planted the seed, and the trouble he ran into on *The 13th Warrior* and *Rollerball* only reinforced his increasing paranoia.

34. Nothing Lasts Forever

The fire on the *Rollerball* set was the breaking point. It's simple to see how McTiernan wound up searching for more information, and easy to understand why he called Pellicano.

McTiernan's subsequent decade-long gauntlet of court cases changed him on a fundamental level. He had always identified as a Republican, but the egalitarian nature of his films and the friendships he sustained throughout the years suggests his conservatism is more fiscal than social. Once he became an enemy of the state, and a target for power-hungry prosecutors, he began to see how a narrow swath of powerful people controlled society. He tried to expose the wrongdoings with his Karl Rove documentary, but not enough people were listening to him in 2008. So he grew jaded, angry, and before long John McTiernan transitioned from celebrated filmmaker to prison inmate.

If anything positive came from McTiernan's incarceration, it was the empathy he found among those marginalized members of society, and his belief in American exceptionalism dissipated. Unfortunately, McTiernan's prison stint may have also transformed him from a confident Alpha male into a man desperate to hang on to the things he worked hard to own. This desperation may have created a convoluted world of future projects, none of which have materialized to this point.

"Red Squad" was probably the closest McTiernan has been to making an honest-to-goodness feature film in the past fourteen years. Since the poster was revealed featuring McTiernan's name, however, Hannibal Pictures has issued a press release listing the new directors as Alexander Witt and David Sardi. The two stars: Nicolas Cage, who has come back on board, and John Travolta.

John McTiernan will be back, in one form or another. He will turn the video-game trailers into a career resurgence, though that resurgence may never find its way back to Hollywood. He could surprise everyone with his Doolittle Raid film in the next few months, or maybe years. But even if McTiernan never makes another film, he will be remembered by action-movie fans for the way he brought depth to the much-maligned genre, as demonstrated in *Predator* and, especially, in *Die Hard*. He will never have *The Hunt for Red October* stricken from his list of credits. And he will be lauded for pulling off a near-impossible feat by remaking—and improving upon—Norman Jewison's *The Thomas Crown Affair*.

True, he will also have three monumental failures attached to his name. Those are not things to run from, however; two of the films have found recent fan acceptance, partly because of their massive flaws. They are the big swings and misses that helped shape the tumultuous career of John McTiernan, and are as much a part of him as John McClane.

Nothing lasts forever. Except history.

Chapter Notes

Introduction

1. Jean-Luc Godard was in line to direct *Bonnie and Clyde* at one point, and François Truffaut did some work on the screenplay.
2. According to Britannica.com, Auteur Theory, derived from Astruc's elucidation of the concept of caméra-stylo ("camera-pen"), holds that the director, who oversees all audio and visual elements of the motion picture, is more to be considered the "author" of the movie than is the writer of the screenplay.
3. Black was the screenwriter, but Richard Donner was the director. *Lethal Weapon*, though, is often cited as the launching pad for Black, who cornered the market on the buddy action formula.

Chapter 1

1. Fellini's *8½* was released a decade prior to *Day for Night*, in 1963.
2. The fully translated English title of Truffaut's film is often referred to as *I Want You to Meet Pamela*.
3. Isabella is not McTiernan's daughter with Carol Land, but the daughter of Anna Maria Monticelli, who plays Pierce Brosnan's wife in *Nomads*, and with whom McTiernan was involved. Land and McTiernan would divorce, but remain professionally involved on the productions of *Die Hard* and *The Hunt for Red October*. Monticelli and McTiernan never married.

Chapter 2

1. While ARC would never be confused with Paramount or Universal, the mid–80s saw the production company at their peak with the success of the 1985 comedy *Teen Wolf*.
2. *Boxcar Bertha* was Martin Scorsese's first film, a director-for-hire-type picture before he directed *Mean Streets*.
3. Lesley-Anne Down, "Interview," *Nomads*, DVD (Los Angeles: Shout! Factory, 2015).
4. "Nomads," boxofficemojo.com.
5. Roger Ebert, "Confusing 'Nomads' Goes Nowhere/Eskimo Legend Grounds Brosnan's Film Debut," *Chicago Sun-Times*, March 10, 1986.

Chapter 3

1. Pete Keely, "Guns and (Shea) Butter: An Oral History of 'Predator,'" *The Hollywood Reporter*, June 21, 2017.

Chapter Notes

2. Arnold Schwarzenegger, *Total Recall: My Unbelievably True Life Story* (New York: Simon & Schuster, 2012), 334.
3. John McTiernan, "Audio Commentary," *Predator*, Ultimate Hunter Edition, DVD (Beverly Hills: 20th Century–Fox Home Entertainment, 2010).
4. According to Box Office Mojo, *Lethal Weapon* was the ninth-highest-grossing movie of 1987, bringing in $65.2 million. Adjusted for 2017 dollars, that's over $147 million.
5. Ventura would be the third cast member to enter politics later in life, winning the gubernatorial seat in Minnesota in 1998. Schwarzenegger was, of course, the governor of California from 2003 to 2011, and Landham tried his hand at Kentucky politics in the 2000s, running for U.S. Senate in 2008. He was removed from the ticket shortly thereafter because of defamatory remarks he made towards the Arab community.

Chapter 4

1. Ryan Lambie, "When Jean-Claude Van Damme Played 'Predator,'" Den of Geek, June 12, 2016, Web.
2. That same year, Kevin Peter Hall could be seen playing the Sasquatch, Harry, in the family comedy *Harry and The Hendersons*.

Chapter 5

1. Arnold's weight loss was more by design prior to filming. He wanted to appear leaner and more agile, as he felt Dutch would be. Regardless, Schwarzenegger didn't eat or drink the water or eat local food during the shoot.
2. Jody Duncan, *The Winston Effect: The Art & History of Stan Winston Studio* (London: Titan Books, 2006).
3. From the *Predator* audio commentary.
4. The mud was actually potter's clay, which was no better than regular mud when it got cold and wet.
5. According to Box Office Mojo, *Beverly Hills Cop II* had the highest opening-weekend with just over $33 million (a four-day weekend, Memorial Day run). *Predator* opened with a little over $12 million.

Chapter 7

1. "The Extreme Sport of Being John McTiernan," *Movieline*, 2001.

Chapter 8

1. John Thurber, "Roderick Thorp; Writer of 'Die Hard,' 'The Detective'" (obituary), *Los Angeles Times*, May 2, 1999.
2. William C. Martell, *The Secrets of Action Screenwriting* (Studio City, CA: First Strike Productions, 2011).
3. Brian Abram, *Die Hard: An Oral History* (Amazon Digital Services, 2016).
4. Three years later, *The Last Boy Scout* would go on to be a Tony Scott movie starring none other than Bruce Willis, working opposite Damon Wayans.
5. *Blind Date* opened number one at the box office, and pulled in an impressive $39.3 million in its theatrical run. Courtesy Box Office Mojo.

Chapter Notes

6. Alan Rickman won the 1987 Best Lead Actor Tony for his portrayal of Valmont in *Dangerous Liaisons*.
7. "Alan Rickman Biography," Biography.com.
8. This quote comes from the 2015 BAFTA celebration of the actor's career.

Chapter 9

1. John McTiernan and Jackson De Govia, "Commentaries," *Die Hard: With a Vengeance*, Nakatomi Plaza Collection, DVD (Beverly Hills: 20th Century–Fox Home Entertainment, 2010).

Chapter 11

1. Jonathan Hensleigh, John McTiernan, and Tom Sherak, "Commentaries," *Die Hard: With a Vengeance*, Nakatomi Plaza Collection, DVD (Beverly Hills: 20th Century–Fox Home Entertainment, 2010).
2. Roger Ebert, "Script Adornments Shoot 'Die Hard' in the Foot," *Chicago Sun-Times*, July 15, 1988, web.
3. "Die Hard," Boxofficemojo.com.

Chapter 12

1. Harlin's work on *A Nightmare on Elm Street 4: The Dream Master*, the highest-grossing film in that franchise, was primarily responsible for getting him the *Die Hard 2* job.
2. "Beneath the Surface: The Making of 'The Hunt for Red October,'" *The Hunt for Red October*, DVD (Hollywood: Paramount Home Entertainment, 2003).
3. That Western turned out to be *Dances with Wolves*, and Costner would win both Best Director and Best Picture at the 63rd Annual Academy Awards in 1991.
4. Bob Thomas, "Submarine Thriller Surfaces with Connery in Command," *Lawrence Journal-World*, March 7, 1990.
5. "The Hunt for Red October," *Siskel & Ebert & The Movies*, CBS-TV, March 1990.
6. "The Hunt for Red October," Boxofficemojo.com.

Chapter 13

1. Nick Setchfield, "Command Performance," *SFX Magazine*, June 2016.

Chapter 14

1. "The Extreme Sport of Being John McTiernan," movieline.com.
2. "First Come, First Served," *The Economist*, July 17, 1997.
3. Danny Leigh, "Lorraine Bracco on 'Goodfellas,' Therapy, and Almost Turning Down 'The Sopranos,'" *The Guardian*, February 20, 2017.
4. "Medicine Man," Boxofficemojo.com.
5. Terry Pristin, "Doctor Sues the Makers of 'The Medicine Man' Film," *Los Angeles Times*, August 18, 1992.

Chapter 15

1. The actual number for *Terminator 2* was $204,122,400. Adjusted for 2017 inflation, the box-office take would be just over $430 million. Courtesy Box Office Mojo.
2. Nick De Semlyan, "The Life and Death of 'Last Action Hero,'" *Empire Online*, January 18, 2012.
3. Boxofficemojo.com.

Chapter 16

1. In the real *Seventh Seal* from 1957, it is Max von Sydow who plays Death.
2. Shane Black, in Nick De Symian, "The Life and Death of 'Last Action Hero.'"

Chapter 17

1. Jonathan Hensleigh, John McTiernan, Tom Sherak, "Commentaries," *Die Hard: With a Vengeance*, Nakatomi Plaza Collection, DVD (Beverly Hills: 20th Century–Fox Home Entertainment, 2010).
2. The *Troubleshooter* screenplay was eventually turned into *Speed 2: Cruise Control*.
3. "Die Hard with a Vengeance," Boxofficemojo.com.

Chapter 19

1. From "First Come, First Served," *The Economist*, July 17, 1997.

Chapter 20

1. Crichton was so popular that in 1994 he became the only artist to ever have number-one sellers in film, television, and publishing with *Jurassic Park*, *ER*, and *Disclosure*, respectively.
2. Ali Gray, "Revisiting 'The 13th Warrior,' the Biggest Flop of All Time," Yahoo! Movies, April 16, 2014.
3. Goldsmith was nominated for an Academy Award a staggering seventeen times during his career. He won his only Oscar of that group in 1977 for his work on *The Omen*.
4. Despite the fact that Cloke took over the role, and Susan Willis has not one minute of screen time in the final theatrical cut of *The 13th Warrior*, Willis remained credited in the role.
5. "The 13th Warrior," Boxofficemojo.com.

Chapter 21

1. Ignatiy Vishnevetsky, "Vikings Fight Cavemen in One of Hollywood's Biggest Flops," *The A.V. Club*, May 8, 2015.

Chapter 22

1. John McTiernan, "Audio Commentary," *The Thomas Crown Affair*, DVD (Beverly Hills: 20th Century–Fox Home Entertainment, 2010).

2. If you notice, the two different establishing shots of the museum's exterior have different banners. The museum had changed exhibits in between these second-unit shots.
3. "The Thomas Crown Affair," Boxofficemojo.com.

Chapter 23

1. Adrian Lyne made a career out of directing erotic thrillers like *9½ Weeks, Fatal Attraction, Indecent Proposal,* and *Unfaithful.*

Chapter 24

1. "McTiernan v. Scott," FindLaw.com.
2. Harry Knowles, "'Rollerball' (2001) Test Print Review," *Ain't It Cool News*, June 7, 2001.
3. "The Extreme Sport of Being John McTiernan."
4. "Shot in Montréal 2000," sympatico.ca, n. d.
5. "Fire on 'Rollerball' Set," SciFi.com, n. d.
6. Eventually, Knowles's influence landed him a fill-in job on Roger Ebert's television review show after Ebert's partner, Gene Siskel, died of brain cancer in 1999.
7. "Rollerball," Boxofficemojo.com.

Chapter 25

1. "Basic Instinct," boxofficemojo.com.
2. Ali Jaafar, "Deadline Distruptors: King of Cannes Mario Kassar on the Glory Days of Carolco, Why Buying Arnie a Plane Made Sense & Talking Vaginas," *Deadline*, May 12, 2016.

Chapter 26

1. The Oscar nomination for *Saturday Night Fever* was technically in 1978, but the nominations were for 1977 movies. Travolta lost his 1994 bid for Best Actor to Tom Hanks for *Forrest Gump.*
2. The vast majority of the *Swordfish* publicity ahead of the film's release centered around Berry's rumored $500,000 paycheck for the single topless shot.
3. John McTiernan, "Director's Commentary," *Basic*, DVD (Culver City, CA: TriStar Home Entertainment, 2003).
4. "Basic," Boxofficemojo.com.

Chapter 27

1. Law Offices of Nancy J. Bickford, APC, "Valuing Goodwill in a Divorce; If You or Your Spouse Is a Creative Professional, There May Be a Twist," San Diego Divorce Attorney's Blog, February 22, 2011.
2. Geoffrey Johnson, "How a Chicago Detective Found the Stolen Body of Elizabeth Taylor's Third Husband, Mike Todd," *Chicago Magazine Online*, March 24, 2011.
3. Dan Glaister, "The Pellicano Files," *The Guardian*, April 19, 2006.

4. Christine Pelisek, "Anthony Pellicano: The Hollywood Phone Hacker Breaks His Silence," *Newsweek*, August 7, 2011.
5. "The Man Who Bagged the Pelican," *The Smoking Gun*, August 7, 2007.
6. Brian Burrough and John Connolly, "Talk of the Town," *Vanity Fair*, January 1, 2008.
7. Michael Hastings, "Exclusive: The Tragic Imprisonment of John McTiernan, Hollywood Icon," *Buzzfeed*, May 24, 2013.
8. Nikki Finke, "Pellicano Prosecutor: Hollywood Wannabe!" *Deadline*, May 6, 2006.
9. Nikki Finke, "EXCLUSIVE: Movie Director's Wife Says McTiernan-Roven Had Good Relationship," *Deadline*, April 3, 2006.

Chapter 28

1. From Dan Glaister, "The Pellicano Files," *The Guardian*, April 19, 2006.
2. Donald C. Shields and John F. Cragan, "The Political Profiling of Elected Democratic Officials: When Rhetorical Vision Participation Runs Amok," *ePluribus Media*, February 18, 2007.
3. Michael Cieply, "Director Fights a Case by Making a New Movie," *New York Times*, April 13, 2009.

Chapter 29

1. "Amazonas Film Festival," IMDb.com.
2. "A Tribute to Director Bill Duke," *Directors Guild of America*, February 23, 2010.
3. "Director John McTiernan Headed to Prison," *Deadline*, October 4, 2010.
4. Alex Ben Block, "'Die Hard' Director John McTiernan Headed to Prison After Supreme Court Denies Appeal," *The Hollywood Reporter*, January 15, 2013.
5. "The Camel Wars," *Turner Classic Movies*, 2010.
6. Pamela McClinctock, "Helmer Makes 'Exchange,'" *Variety*, June 4, 2006.
7. Scott Weinberg, "John McTiernan to Helm Chase-Heavy Action-Thriller 'Run,'" *Moviefone*, May 23, 2007.
8. Ross Miller, "John McTiernan to Direct Action-Thriller 'Shrapnel,'" *Screen Rant*, September 10, 2010.

Chapter 30

1. "FPC Yankton," BOP.gov.
2. Brad Bird, who directed *The Incredibles* and *Mission: Impossible—Ghost Protocol*, actually penned an article in *Rolling Stone* in February 2013, discussing the impact *Die Hard* had on his own career.
3. Richard George Kopf, "Ghost Dope, Statutory Minimum Sentences in Drug Cases, Judge Jed Rakoff, U.S. Sen. Charles Grassley, Chairman of the Senate Judiciary Committee, and the Des Moines Register Editorial," *Hercules and the Umpire*, December 12, 2015.
4. Eriq Gardner, "Director John McTiernan Wants to Make a 'Thomas Crown' Sequel to Fight Bank Liquidation," *The Hollywood Reporter*, October 14, 2015.

Chapter 31

1. Alex Ben Block, "'Die Hard' Director John McTiernan Released from Prison," *The Hollywood Reporter*, February 25, 2014.

2. Hannibalpictures.com.
3. Dave McNary, "McTiernan to Direct DEA Thriller 'Red Squad,'" *Empire Online*, February 7, 2014.
4. Eriq Gardner, "'Die Hard' Director John McTiernan Reveals Next Film Projects at Bankruptcy Hearing," *The Hollywood Reporter*, August 29, 2014.
5. Eriq Gardner, "Director John McTiernan Wants to Make a 'Thomas Crown' Sequel to Fight Bank Liquidation," *The Hollywood Reporter*, October 14, 2015.

Chapter 32

1. Dave McNary, "Michael B. Jordan Starring in 'Thomas Crown Affair' Remake," *Variety*, February 24, 2016.
2. Sam Barsanti, "'Die Hard' Director John McTiernan Calls Superhero Movies 'Fascist,'" *A.V. Club*, July 13, 2016.

Chapter 33

1. Tatiana Siegel, "What Happened to 'Die Hard' Director John McTiernan?" *The Hollywood Reporter*, June 27, 2016.
2. Fergus Ryan, "'Die Hard' Director John McTiernan to Shoot WWII Film in China," *China Film Insider*, November 1, 2016.

Bibliography

Abram, Brian. *Die Hard: An Oral History*. Amazon Digital Services, 2016.
Barsanti, Sam. "'Die Hard' Director John McTiernan Calls Superhero Movies 'Fascist.'" *A.V. Club*, July 13, 2016.
"Beneath the Surface: The Making of 'The Hunt for Red October.'" *The Hunt for Red October*, DVD (Hollywood: Paramount Home Entertainment, 2003).
Biography.com.
Block, Alex Ben. "'Die Hard' Director John McTiernan Headed to Prison After Supreme Court Denies Appeal." *The Hollywood Reporter*, January 15, 2013.
_____. "'Die Hard' Director John McTiernan Released From Prison." *The Hollywood Reporter*, February 25, 2014.
Boxofficemojo.com.
Burrough, Brian, and John Connolly. "Talk of The Town." *Vanity Fair*, January 1, 2008.
Cieply, Michael. "Director Fights a Case by Making a New Movie." *New York Times*, April 13, 2009.
"The Camel Wars." Turner Classic Movies, 2010.
De Semlyan, Nick. "The Life and Death of 'Last Action Hero.'" *Empire Online*, January 18, 2012.
"Director John McTiernan Headed to Prison." *Deadline*, October 4, 2010.
Down, Leslie-Ann. "Interview," *Nomads*, DVD (Los Angeles: Shout! Factory, 2015).
Duncan, Jody. *The Winston Effect: The Art & History of Stan Winston Studio*. London: Titan Books, 2006.
Ebert, Roger. "Confusing 'Nomads' Goes Nowhere / Eskimo Legend Grounds Brosnan's Film Debut." *Chicago Sun-Times*, March 10, 1986.
_____. "Script Adornments Shoot 'Die Hard' in the Foot." *Chicago Sun-Times*, July 15, 1988.
"The Extreme Sport of Being John McTiernan." *Movieline*, 2001.
Finke, Nikki. "EXCLUSIVE: Movie Director's Wife Says McTiernan-Roven Had Good Relationship," *Deadline*, April 3, 2006.
_____. "Pellicano Prosecutor: Hollywood Wannabe!" *Deadline*, May 6, 2006.
"Fire on 'Rollerball' Set." SciFi.com, n. d.
"First Come, First Served." *The Economist*, July 17, 1997.
Gardner, Eriq. "'Die Hard' Director John McTiernan Reveals Next Film Projects at Bankruptcy Hearing." *The Hollywood Reporter*, August 29, 2014.
_____. "Director John McTiernan Wants to Make a 'Thomas Crown' Sequel to Fight Bank Liquidation." *The Hollywood Reporter*, October 14, 2015.
Glaister, Dan. "The Pellicano Files." *The Guardian*, April 19, 2006.
Gray, Ali. "Revisiting 'The 13th Warrior,' the Biggest Flop of All Time." Yahoo! Movies, April 16, 2014.

Bibliography

Hannibalclassics.com.
Hannibalpictures.com.
Hastings, Michael. "Exclusive: The Tragic Imprisonment of John McTiernan, Hollywood Icon." *Buzzfeed*, May 24, 2013.
Hensleigh, Jonathan, John McTiernan, and Tom Sherak. "Commentaries," *Die Hard: With a Vengeance*, Nakatomi Plaza Collection, DVD (Beverly Hills: 20th Century–Fox Home Entertainment, 2010).
"The Hunt for Red October." *Siskel & Ebert & the Movies*, CBS-TV, March 3, 1990.
IMDb.com.
Keely, Pete. "Guns and (Shea) Butter: An Oral History of 'Predator.'" *The Hollywood Reporter*, June 21, 2017.
Jaafar, Ali. "Deadline Disruptors: King of Cannes Mario Kassar on the Glory Days of Carolco, Why Buying Arnie a Plane Made Sense & Talking Vaginas." *Deadline*, May 12, 2016.
Johnson, Geoffrey. "How a Chicago Detective Found the Stolen Body of Elizabeth Taylor's Third Husband, Mike Todd." *Chicago Magazine Online*, March 24, 2011.
Knowles, Harry. "'Rollerball' (2001) Test Print Review." *Ain't It Cool News*, June 7, 2001.
Kopf, Richard George. "Ghost Dope, Statutory Minimum Sentences in Drug Cases, Judge Jed Rakoff, U.S. Sen. Charles Grassley, Chairman of the Senate Judiciary Committee, and the Des Moines Register Editorial." *Hercules and the Umpire*, December 12, 2015.
Lambie, Ryan. "When Jean-Claude Van Damme Played Predator." Den of Geek, June 12, 2016.
Law Offices of Nancy J. Bickford, APC. "Valuing Goodwill in a Divorce; If You or Your Spouse Is a Creative Professional, There May Be a Twist." San Diego Divorce Attorney's Blog, February 22, 2011.
Leigh, Danny. "Lorraine Bracco on 'Goodfellas,' Therapy, and Almost Turning Down 'The Sopranos.'" *The Guardian*, February 20, 2017.
"The Man Who Bagged the Pelican." *The Smoking Gun*, August 7, 2007.
Martell, William C. *The Secrets of Action Screenwriting*. Studio City, CA: First Strike Productions, 2011.
McClintock, Pamela. "Helmer Makes 'Exchange.'" *Variety*, June 4, 2006.
McNary, Dave. "McTiernan to Direct DEA Thriller 'Red Squad.'" *Empire Online*, February 7, 2014.
_____. "Michael B. Jordan Starring in 'Thomas Crown Affair' Remake." *Variety*, February 24, 2016.
McTiernan, John. "Audio Commentary." *Predator*, Ultimate Hunter Edition, DVD (Beverly Hills: 20th Century–Fox Home Entertainment, 2010).
_____. "Audio Commentary." *The Thomas Crown Affair*, DVD (Beverly Hills: 20th Century–Fox Home Entertainment, 2010).
_____. "Director's Commentary." *Basic*, DVD (Culver City, CA: TriStar Home Entertainment, 2003).
McTiernan, John, and Jackson De Govi. "Commentaries." *Die Hard: With a Vengeance*, Nakatomi Plaza Collection, DVD (Beverly Hills: 20th Century–Fox Home Entertainment, 2010).
Miller, Ross. "John McTiernan to Direct Action-Thriller 'Shrapnel.'" *Screen Rant*, September 10, 2010.
Pelisek, Christine. "Anthony Pellicano: The Hollywood Phone Hacker Breaks His Silence." *Newsweek*, August 7, 2011.
Pristin, Terry. "Doctor Sues the Makers of 'The Medicine Man' Film." *Los Angeles Times*, August 18, 1992.
Ryan, Fergus. "'Die Hard' Director John McTiernan to Shoot WWII Film in China." *China Film Insider*, November 1, 2016.

Schwarzenegger, Arnold. *Total Recall: My Unbelievably True Life Story*. New York: Simon & Schuster, 2012.
Setchfield, Nick. "Command Performance." *SFX Magazine*, June 2016.
Shields, Donald C., and John F. Cragan. "The Political Profiling of Elected Democratic Officials: When Rhetorical Vision Participation Runs Amok." *ePluribus Media*, February 18, 2007.
"Shot in Montréal 2000," sympatico.ca, n. d.
Siegel, Tatiana. "What Happened to 'Die Hard' Director John McTiernan?" *The Hollywood Reporter*, June 27, 2016.
Thomas, Bob. "Submarine Thriller Surfaces with Connery in Command." *Lawrence Journal-World*, March 7, 1990.
Thurber, John. "Roderick Thorp; Writer of 'Die Hard,' 'The Detective'" (obituary). *Los Angeles Times*, May 2, 1999.
"A Tribute to Director Bill Duke." Directors Guild of America, February 23, 2010.
Vishnevetsky, Ignatiy. "Vikings Fight Cavemen in One of Hollywood's Biggest Flops." *A.V. Club*, May 8, 2015.
Weinberg, Scott. "John McTiernan to Helm Chase-Heavy Action-Thriller 'Run.'" *Moviefone*, May 23, 2007.

John McTiernan Filmography

Nomads (1986), Cinema VII
Predator (1987), 20th Century–Fox
Die Hard (1988), 20th Century–Fox
The Hunt for Red October (1990), Paramount Pictures
Medicine Man (1992), Touchstone Pictures
Last Action Hero (1993), Columbia Pictures
Die Hard with a Vengeance (1995), 20th Century–Fox
The Thomas Crown Affair (1999), MGM Studios
The 13th Warrior (1999), Touchstone Pictures
Rollerball (2002), MGM Pictures
Basic (2003), Columbia Pictures

Index

Abraham, F. Murray 93
Ackland, Joss 75
Ain't It Cool News 150–151; *see also* Knowles, Harry
Allen, Woody 89; *see also The Purple Rose of Cairo*
American Film Institute (AFI) 12–16, 194
The Angel Levine 14
ARC 17
Arnott, David 91, 93, 94, 149

Baldwin, Alec 72, 73, 77, 81, 178
Banderas, Antonio 120–122, 125, 127
Basic 155–160, 163, 168, 175, 176, 178, 197
Basic Instinct 2 153–155; *see also* Stone, Sharon
Basinger, Kim 50
Baxley, Craig R. 36
Bear Claw 81, 117; *see also* Wyoming
Bedelia, Bonnie 52, 57, 148; *see also Heart Like a Wheel*
Beowulf 120, 123, 126
Bird, Brad 178
Black, Shane 6, 26, 49, 91, 93, 94, 102, 106, 149; *see also The Last Boy Scout; Lethal Weapon*
Blainville fire 149
Bochner, Hart 53, 56
Bracco, Lorraine 82–84, 195
Brandauer, Klaus Maria 73
Bratt, Benjamin 154
Brosnon, Pierce 17–20, 128, 130–132, 134, 135, 137, 138
Burch, Jackie 30, 52, 53
Busch, Anita 165, 166, 171; *see also Los Angeles Times*

The Camel Wars 176
Cameron, James 6, 7, 31, 33, 90, 102; *see also The Terminator; Terminator 2: Judgment Day*

Canton, Mark 92
Carnahan, Joe 178
Carney, Art 93
Carrillo, Elpidia 28
Castner, Elliott 16
Chavez, Richard 27
Clancy, Tom 70–72, 77, 79, 81, 119, 144, 191, 195
Cloke, Kristen 123
Columbia Pictures 90–93, 95, 96, 198
Computer Generated Imagery (CGI) 90, 125, 184
Connery, Sean 73–75, 82–84
Conti, Bill 18
Costner, Kevin 72, 123, 125
Cragan, John 172
Crichton, Michael 119, 120, 122, 123, 125; *see also Eaters of the Dead*
Cronenweth, Jeff 192
Curry, Tim 74, 75

Dance, Charles 93, 100
Davis, John 24
Day for Night 14, 15; *see also* Truffaut, François
Deadly Exchange 176
de Bont, Jan 55, 74
DeGovia, Jackson 58
DeLorean, John 164
The Demon's Daughter 16
de Souza, Steven E. 49, 51
DeSymlian, Nick 102
The Detective 47, 49, 50; *see also* Thorp, Roderick
De Vito, Danny 94
Diaz, Olivier 168
Die Hard 49, 50, 52–55, 57–65, 69, 70, 74, 77, 78, 91, 102, 104–106, 111–114, 127, 148, 168, 169, 178, 192, 195, 199
Die Hard 2: Die Harder (Die Hard 2) 61, 70, 112, 113

Index

Die Hard: With a Vengeance 105–108, 111–114, 117, 119, 127, 132, 156, 178, 196
Diggs, Taye 157
Dixon, Leslie 130
Dolly track 133
The Doolittle Raid 191, 199
Douglas, Gordon 47
Dowd, Ned 120
Down, Leslie-Ann 18–20
Dubrow, Donna 69, 81, 117–119, 143, 163, 168, 183, 185, 198
Duke, Bill 27, 174
Dunaway, Faye 129, 130, 132, 137, 138

Eaters of the Dead 119–122, 196; see also Crichton, Michael
Ebert, Roger 20, 64, 77, 111; see also Siskel, Gene; Siskel and Ebert
"Extremely Violent" 89–91

Ferguson, Larry 71, 72, 92, 144, 145
Ferguson, William H. 84
Fields, Bert 164
Fischer, Dale (Judge Fischer) 175, 176
Fisher, Carrie 92, 94
Folsey, George, Jr. 159
French New Wave 1, 13–15

Garner, James 50
Gérardmer International Fantastic Film Festival 174
Ghost Recon 192; see also *The Red Dot*
Gleason, Paul 53, 64
Glenn, Scott 74
Goldman, William 91, 92, 94
Goldsmith, Jerry 122
A Good Day to Die Hard 61, 113, 114
Gordon, Lawrence (Larry) 23, 24, 52, 63
Grey, Brad 164
Gudunov, Alexander 53

Hall, Kevin Peter 33, 35, 36
Hannibal Pictures (Hannibal Classics) 183, 184, 187, 192
Harlin, Renny 70, 106, 112–114
Harrington, Kate 140, 143, 148, 163, 169, 175
Harrison, William 143
Heart Like a Wheel 52, 148; see also Bedelia, Bonnie
Hensleigh, Jonathan 104–107, 110
Hill, Walter 23, 24, 26
Hockeimer, Henry 168, 182
The Hunt for Red October 70, 71, 73–75, 76–82, 92, 125, 126, 134, 144, 169, 178, 192, 195, 199

Irons, Jeremy 107, 178

Jackson, Samuel L. 106, 107, 109, 111, 156–158, 178
Jellis, James 185, 186
Jewison, Norman 128, 130, 136, 143, 144; see also *Rollerball* (1975); *The Thomas Crown Affair* (1968)
Jones, William 133
Judgment at Nuremburg 76
Juilliard 12
Jurassic Park 92, 95, 96, 102, 119, 120, 198; see also Spielberg, Steven

Kadár, Ján 13, 14, 55, 77, 194; see also *The Angel Levine*; *Lies My Father Told Me*; *The Shop on Main Street*
Kael, Pauline 129
Kaman, Michael 54
Klein, Chris 146, 149, 151
Knowles, Harry 150, 151, 153; see also Ain't It Cool News
Kulich, Vladimir 121

Lambro, Phillip 84
Land, Carol 12
Landham, Sonny 26, 27
Last Action Hero 91–98, 101–103, 105, 149, 196–198
The Last Boy Scout 49, 91, 106; see also Black, Shane
"The Last Days of Eden" 82; see also *Medicine Man*
Leary, Denis 132, 134, 139
Leff, Adam 89–91, 98, 103
Lethal Weapon 6, 12, 91, 104, 132; see also Black, Shane
Lies My Father Told Me 14; see also Kádar, Ján
Link, John F. 55
Live Free or Die Hard 61, 112, 113
LL Cool J 146, 149
Los Angeles Times 165; see also Busch, Anita

Mad Max: Fury Road 190, 196
McAlpine, Donald 34, 38, 55, 83
McCorkle, Pat 147
McKellan, Ian 93, 101
McQueen, Steve 129, 130, 137
McTiernan, John Sr. 11
McTiernan, Myra 11
McTiernan, Truman Elizabeth 143
Medicine Man 69, 82–84, 195, 196; see also "Last Days of Eden"; *The Stand*
Meditation 16
MGM 130, 143, 150, 151, 153, 155
Moore, Chris 90

212

Index

Neill, Sam 74, 75
Neufeld, Mace 71–73
Nielsen, Connie 157–159
Nomads 16–20, 24, 25, 128, 130, 180
Noonan, Tom 93, 94, 98
Norris, Chuck 1, 5, 6, 89
Nothing Lasts Forever 48, 49, 54; see also Thorp, Roderick

O'Brien, Austin 92
Ovitz, Michael 164, 165, 167

Paramount Pictures 71, 72, 80, 183
Patterson, Daniel 166
Pellicano, Anthony 163–168, 171, 174–176, 178, 183, 183, 185, 198
Penn, Zak 89–91, 94, 98, 102
Phillips Exeter 11
Pine, Chris 79, 81
Pogue, John 144, 145
Poor Richard's Almanack 16
Predator 23–30, 32–42, 54, 55, 70, 71, 74, 77, 78, 82, 83, 91, 127, 146, 174, 192, 194, 195, 199
Priestly, Tom 133
Proctor, Alexander 166
Prosky, Robert 93
The Purple Rose of Cairo 89; see also Allen, Woody

Quinn, Anthony 93

The Red Dot 192; see also *Ghost Recon*
Red Squad 184–186, 199
Reeves, Keanu 145, 146
Reno, Jean 148
Revell, Graeme 122, 126
Ribisi, Giovanni 157
Rickman, Alan 51, 52, 59, 60, 61, 65, 105, 107
Rollerball (1975) 143; see also Jewison, Norman
Rollerball (2002) 144–147, 149–151, 153–155, 168–170, 197, 198
Romijn-Stamos, Rebecca 147, 148, 152
Rove, Karl 170, 172, 173, 199
Roven, Charles 144–146, 148, 149, 168–170, 175, 182
Ruehl, Mercedes 93
"Run" 176
Russo, Rene 131, 134, 135, 137–140
Ruthless 193

St. Clair, Beau 130, 131, 144
Saunders, Daniel 166, 168, 169, 171, 198
Schulman, Tom 82–84
Scott, Sam (The Scotts) 117, 118, 143, 168

Schwarzenegger, Arnold 1, 5, 6, 24–27, 29–36, 38, 40, 41, 50, 89–94, 96, 100–102, 146, 149, 165
Seagal, Steven 165
Sharif, Omar 121
Shepherd, Cybil 50
Shields, Donald 172
The Shop in Main Street 13, 14; see also Kádar, Ján
shrapnel 176, 183
Silver, Joel 24, 25, 33, 48, 49, 51, 52, 58, 63, 70, 91
"Simon Says" 104, 105
Sinatra, Frank 47, 48
Siskel, Gene 77; see also Ebert, Roger; Siskel and Ebert
Siskel and Ebert 77; see also Ebert, Roger; Siskel, Gene
Sistrunk, Gail (Gail McTiernan) 176–178, 187
The 6th Annual Amazonas Film Festival 174
"The Sleeping Dogs of Amagansett" 188
Sofilm Summercamp 188
Spielberg, Steven 92, 119; see also *Jurassic Park*
Stallone, Sylvester 1, 4–6, 50, 89
The Stand 82; see also *Medicine Man*
State University of New York (SUNY) 12
Stone, Sharon 153, 154; see also *Basic Instinct 2*
Stuart, Jeb 48, 49

Tales of the 22nd Century 16
The Terminator 6, 31; see also Cameron, James
Terminator 2: Judgment Day 90; see also Cameron, James
The 13th Warrior 122–128, 134–136, 151, 196–198
Thomas, Jim (The Thomas Brothers) 23, 24, 26
Thomas, John (The Thomas Brothers) 23, 24, 26
The Thomas Crown Affair (1968) 128–130, 138, 143, 144, 199
The Thomas Crown Affair (1999) 132, 135, 137, 154, 180, 188, 197
"Thomas Crown and the Missing Lioness" 180, 187, 188
Thorp, Roderick 47, 48, 70; see also *The Detective*; *Nothing Lasts Forever*
Touchstone Pictures 120–123
Travolta, John 106, 155–159, 176, 183, 197, 199
Truffaut, François 1, 2, 14, 15; see also *Day for Night* 14, 15

Index

Trustman, Alan 129
20th Century–Fox (Fox) 23–25, 34, 37, 47, 48, 57, 63, 102, 104, 105, 109, 183

Urioste, Frank J. 55

Vallone, John 29
Vance, Courtney B. 74
Van Damme, Jean-Claude 29–32, 34
Vanderbilt, James 155
Van Holt, Brian 157
VelJohnson, Reginald 53, 106
Ventura, Jesse 27, 35, 39

"Warbirds" 183–186
Wasser, Dennis 168
Weathers, Carl 25, 26, 35, 38, 40, 146, 174

Weitzman, Howard 164
White, DeVoreaux 57
Willis, Bruce 50–52, 57, 59, 60, 63, 65, 70, 72, 106–109, 111–113, 196
Willis, Susan 123
Wilson, David Campbell 144, 150
Wimmer, Kurt 130
Winston, Stan 31–33, 35
Wright, John 122
Wyoming 143, 168, 170, 181, 182, 185, 187, 188, 198; *see also* Bear Claw

Yankton Federal Prison Camp (Yankton Prison Camp) 177, 180

Zunino, Mark 140

www.ingramcontent.com/pod-product-compliance
Ingram Content Group UK Ltd.
Pitfield, Milton Keynes, MK11 3LW, UK
UKHW041956140426
5217IPUK00015B/833